European Business Law and Practice Series

Corporate Acquisitions and Mergers in Portugal

A Practical Guide to the Legal, Financial and Administrative Implications

Other Titles in the Series

Concentration Control in the European Economic Community, P.V.F. Bos, J. Stuyck, P. Wytinck
(ISBN 1-85333-570-3)

European Community Telecommunications Regulation, S. Mosteshar
(ISBN 1-85333-756-0)

Harmonization and Hazard: Regulating Workplace Health and Safety in the European Community, R. Baldwin, T. Daintith (eds.)
(ISBN 1-85333-723-4)

Intellectual Property and the Internal Market of the European Community, P. Groves, A. Martino, C. Miskin, J. Richards
(ISBN 1-85333-575-4)

Privatization in Central and Eastern Europe, P. Šarčević (ed.)
(ISBN 1-85333-713-7)

(*Please order by title or ISBN*)

European Business Law and Practice Series

Corporate Acquisitions and Mergers in Portugal

A Practical Guide to the Legal, Financial and Administrative Implications

Ronald Charles Wolf

Graham & Trotman
A member of Wolters Kluwer Academic Publishers
LONDON/DORDRECHT/BOSTON

Graham & Trotman Limited
Sterling House
66 Wilton Road
London SW1V 1DE
UK

Kluwer Academic Publishers Group
101 Philip Drive
Assinippi Park
Norwell, MA 02061
USA

First published 1993

British Library Cataloguing in Publication Data

A catalogue record for this book is available from the British Library

ISBN 1 85333 793 5
Series ISBN 1 85333 714 5

Library of Congress CIP data
Wolf, Ronald Charles.
Corporate acquisitions and mergers in Portugal : a practical guide to the legal, financial, and administrative implications / Ronald Charles Wolf.
p. cm.
Includes index.
ISBN 1-85333-793-5
1. Consolidation and merger of corporations—Portugal. I. Title.
KKQ1148.W64 1993
346.496'06626—dc20
[344.69066626] 93-12418
CIP

Typeset by Tradespools Ltd, Frome, Somerset
Printed and bound in Great Britain by Athenaeum Press Ltd.,
Newcastle-upon-Tyne

Contents

Preface

The first time Marilyn and I saw Lisbon, I recall a shimmering white light—for it was July 1968—and the only relief was the coolness of the blue river Tagus which slowly wound its way past Commerce Square on its path to the nearby ocean. Lisbon was little more than a market town and the brightness we saw was the same reflected light you would see from a distance in any oasis, for Lisbon was not only the port of entry into Portugal but also Europe, a hilled town with ancient fortifications and aqueducts, palm trees scattered haphazardly about, lending conviction to your belief that Lisbon and Portugal were still part of a more remote, distant era.

There was little manufacturing, a lot of cottage industry, a few large land holdings dominating the fertile fields to the east of Lisbon. Porto and the north were more industrialised but the shoe and textile industries were the only significant employers and they could hardly support a national population. The sustenance of life came from the small landholdings that most everyone had, passed down through the family generations. Portugal was in 1968 a country with no particular destiny.

In 1974 this was all changed by a revolution which certainly had an unintended effect. Originally conceived because of military discontent, it quickly became a debate about the type of society which would prevail, and through the efforts of many heroic Portuguese, Portugal's future was determined with the establishment of a republic and democracy, culminating in the country becoming a full member of the Common Market.

Today, Portugal can be proud of a solid economic growth, a

full participant in a growing, united Europe, a working partner in the construction of a free and thriving European continent. A country now with a destiny: substantial foreign investment, modernisation of industry and services, full employment.

I have almost written this book partially out of a duty to those many Portuguese who never lost faith in their country and in the fervour of the 1974 Revolution did not hesitate to break down barricades erected by others who thought democracy had only one and not multiple meanings. Marilyn and I have watched as first the few existing industries were seized by workers, then nationalised, sometimes run by appointed party members, all this giving way to companies being returned to their owners, culminating in the wave of privatisations and the enacting of laws designed to encourage foreign investment and which thrust Portugal fully into the 20th (almost the 21st) century.

The Portugal of today is economically very different from what it was in 1968 and it was also this thought that has prompted me to write this book. My sentiments that Marilyn and I, as Americans living in Portugal, could also make a small contribution in helping others understand what good sense it makes to do business in Portugal.

I have tried to write a readable review of the basic areas of Portuguese law which a foreign investor normally encounters and wishes to know more about. For those, therefore, considering Portugal as a potential investment, this book is a legal and business guide, a practical hand extended to invite you, intellectually, at least, to discover this truly remarkable country that is Portugal.

Casal Do Piolho
Ericeira, Portugal
1993

Portugal

Ronald Charles Wolf

Economic Considerations

Writing in 1572, the epic poet Luis Camoes described Portugal as the place "where the earth ends and the sea begins". Now, 400 years later, with the Golden Age of Discoveries (Magellan, Vasco de Gama) a remote historical fact, a new era has begun for Portugal, symbolised by its past presidency of the Council of Ministers of the European Community from 1st January to June 1992. Situated on the south-western tip of Europe facing the Atlantic Ocean, Portugal has, as a consequence of joining the European Economic Community in 1986, become a gateway for foreign investors wishing to take advantage of the largest international market for goods and services: the EEC.

Since 1974 when a long-running dictatorship was overthrown, historical events in Portugal have transformed what was a country governed by a conservative alliance of various factions into a true democracy. Moreover, in the last election held in October 1991, the right of centre Social Democrats led by Prime Minister Anibal Cavaco Silva obtained a comfortable majority which will take them through to 1995. Consequently, the pro-foreign investment stance of the Social Democrats will continue to be a feature of Portugal's business environment.

Additionally, Portugal joined the European Monetary System (EMS) on 6th April 1992. From April to September 1992, the escudo had been a strong currency, with a permitted trading range of 6.18% against other EMS currencies. On 16th September, the English pound left the European exchange-rate mechanism (ERM). On 23rd November, there was a realignment within the ERM. Although after the realignment there was little change in the value of the escudo against its main trading partners, it is still too early to predict if the escudo will throughout 1993 continue to be a stable currency. It is certainly the intent of the Government as expressed many times through the Minister of Finance. However, one banking study indicates that on purchasing power parities, the escudo is overvalued by almost 4% and hence it is possible that 1993 will see a further devaluation of the escudo. This is certainly the wish of the exporters who have become accustomed to devaluations to maintain their competive position in foreign markets. A number of Portuguese economists have argued that maintaining the escudo at its present level (e.g. DM equals 92 escudos) will result in a rise in unemployment, a loss of foreign markets and a higher internal consumption. Any investment in Portugal should assume as a variable a devaluation of the escudo. In fact, the week of 10th May 1993 witnessed a 3.5% devaluation of the escudo and further devaluations can be expected.

As from 1st January 1993, the Bank of Portugal has completely liberalised the movement of capital. Foreigners can have escudo deposits and participate in the Portuguese monetary market. Non-residents can obtain loans in escudos and have free access to the public debt market. Banks operating in Portugal can also realise operations of purchase and sale of escudos with fixed terms, options and swaps. However, a devaluing escudo has not in the past curtailed foreign investment in Portugal. The table below indicates foreign investment in Portugal from 1980 to 1990.

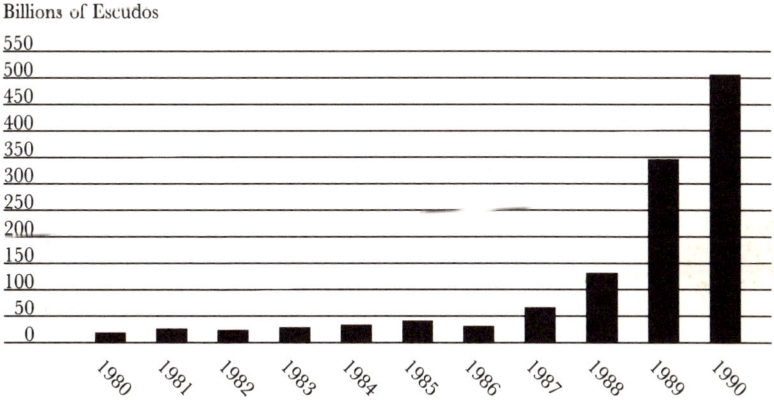

The Republic of Portugal has much to commend it for investors. It is a small country of approximately 90,000 square kilometres. According to the National Institute of Statistics (INE), the population for 1990 was estimated to be 10,393,000. Portuguese is the spoken language and is also the language spoken in the former Portuguese colonies of Angola, Guinea-Bissau, Cape Verde, Macau, Mozambique, São Tomé and Principe and of course in Brazil, which was originally colonised by the Portuguese. In all of these countries where Portuguese is spoken there are still strong cultural and commercial ties with Portugal and the foreign investor who establishes himself in Portugal can expect to do business not only with Portugal's EEC partners, but also with any of these former Portuguese colonies.

The climate of Portugal is mild with no extremes of temperature. The 1991 Census figures of the INE estimate that the capital of Portugal, Lisbon, has a population of 659,649. However, the actual district of Lisbon, which would include all the suburban towns, had a population at 31st December 1989 of 2,130,600. Nevertheless, this only translates into 771 persons per square kilometre. The southern part of Portugal, called the Algarve, has a Mediterranean climate and has for many years enjoyed rapid economic growth due to tourism. In fact, tourism has now spread rapidly throughout Portugal as many visitors discover the natural beauty of a country with a low population density (about 100 inhabitants per square kilometre) and with no large industrial city adjacent to any other. Portugal's second largest city is Porto, with a 1991 INE Census population of 297,506, although, as in the case of Lisbon, there is a large influx of people for purposes of commerce in the multiple suburban towns surrounding Porto.

From the point of view of investment and potential business prospects, the INE has published (1990 figures) statistical reports which are helpful and revealing. From 1986 to 1988, educational institutions increased by 2000 units; the primary sector in Portugal accounted for 17.9% of the whole; the average daily wage in 1989 in Lisbon was 2605 escudos and in Porto 4938 escudos; 1991 May figures published by INE under the rubric of external relations for the first three months of 1991 reveal a reduction in exports and imports, but with an increase in exports to Germany, Belgium, Luxembourg and Spain. In the balance of current account transactions, the 1989 balance in millions of dollars was 139 and for 1990, –61 (minus); however, for January 1990, non-monetary operations showed a slight surplus of 12 million dollars with a substantial positive balance of payments on capital account; this latter fact was due to the injection of a massive amount of foreign funds into Portugal.

Outside Continental Portugal, the autonomous regions of Madeira and the Azores have benefited from special laws affecting their jurisdictions. In Madeira, there is a free trade zone as well as offshore services and tax concessions. Of particular interest is the use of English-type trust companies operating as they do in any offshore centre. Detailed information on Madeira can be obtained from the Madeira

Development Company, Funchal, Madeira. The autonomous region comprising the nine islands of the Azores also has a free trade zone (in Santa Maria) and various tax benefits. Further information can easily be obtained from any of the major Continental Portuguese banks.

For those foreign investors accustomed to a parliamentary democracy, Portugal's political system will be readily understandable. There is a President of the Republic, who is elected to ensure that the democratic institutions function in accordance with the Constitution of 1976. He is the Head of State and Supreme Commander-in-Chief of the Armed Forces.

Although the President in theory appoints the Prime Minister who chooses his ministers, as a practical matter this appointment reflects the choices of the Portuguese people exercised through their electoral votes. The people elect deputies to the National Assembly and the President, in accordance with the election results and following consultations with the political parties, will ask a party (or parties) to form a government. The legislative function of the government is thus confined to the National Assembly, with the President of the Republic representing the nation externally.

Following the enactment of the 1976 Constitution, Portugal went through a period of numerous brief governments involving various multi-party alliances. However, in 1984 the Social Democrats obtained a majority, which was repeated in 1991, and Portugal has since that date been governed with considerable political stability; so much so that during 1991 the Bank of Portugal had to enact monetary measures in an attempt to retard the inflow of foreign currencies which were attracted to the stable, high interest earnings in escudos and since Portugal joined the European Monetary Exchange System in 1992, the Bank of Portugal has had to intervene periodically in an attempt to prevent the escudo from appreciating beyond the EMS parameters.

Civil Law System

Portugal is a country with long-established legal traditions and the Portuguese legal order is classified as a civil code system by comparative law scholars. But this is an over-simplification. At the time of the incipient political foundations of Portugal (about 1140), there was little central political intervention and there existed a common law which in those times regulated a society which, quoting a Portuguese legal scholar, "lived according to the law of God". Research has shown that this common law was a mixture of Roman and German law, both the result of pensinular invasions. Consequently, Portuguese law is not an esoteric, unusual system of law but one where the principles of developed, consensual legal traditions of other civilisations have contributed and it is a legal order whose commercial law principles certainly will be entirely familiar to lawyers from industrialised countries. Its legal institutions have always been independent, judges being career officials who normally start out as young district attorneys. The influence of the common law in present-day courts has been negligible in Portugal, although Portuguese legal scholars are quite familiar with the system of common law and much recent legislation has drawn heavily upon common law experience, particularly in the area of joint ventures.

Probably the most striking difference between the civil code system and the common law for the businessman or international lawyer is the heavy reliance in Portugal on the various codes or decree laws, resulting in legal documents which are invariably quite short by comparison with similar common law documents. The 100-page joint venture agreement in America or England is unlikely to find its counterpart in Portugal. On the other hand, precedent is not ignored in the judicial system. It simply does not have the same binding force as it does in the common law. A past decision in Portugal is persuasive, perhaps a good reason for repeating a principle of law, but the law is very much the letter of the law as written by the legislators. Lawyers in their arguments will cite precedents, judges will refer to them in their opinions, fully annotated collective works of precedent are published, but the entire emphasis is on general principles of law and the conclusions resulting therefrom.

One different aspect of Portuguese law which should be understood by lawyers and business people trained in the Anglo-Saxon tradition is the treatment given to spouses under the Portuguese Civil Code. In Portugal, when you marry, a "regime of marriage" is adopted. In countries following the Anglo-Saxon legal school, marriage normally means separate property. Couples wishing to own things together put their names on the legal instrument at the time of purchase. In Portugal, unless another arrangment is made, all property acquired after the marriage (unless by gift or inheritance) belongs to both spouses, no matter who sign the deed of purchase. If husband purchases shares of stock, in theory they belong to both the husband and wife, since they were acquired after the marriage. Real estate purchased by a husband, under his own signature, cannot thereafter be sold by him alone, since at the time of purchase, the notary, in the deed, will recite the regime of marriage. Consequently, on all commercial transactions, other than acts of mere administration, the power of any spouse to act alone must be examined. It is possible to be married with separate property, just as it is possible to be married with general community property (more broad than acquired property) but these regimes must be specifically adopted at the time of marriage.

Agency Agreements, Distribution Contracts and Consortiums

While many foreign investors launch a business enterprise in Portugal without any prior national experience, many such ventures are often preceded by trial experiences which may last several years, e.g. an agency agreement or distribution contract or even a specific project which enables the foreign investor to appreciate at first hand the business atmosphere of Portugal, such as the formation of a consortium.

Agency Agreements

The contract of agency, or commercial representation as it is also described in Portuguese law, is regulated by Decree Law 178/86 of 3rd July 1986 as amended by Decree Law 118/93 of 13th April 1993. Prior to that date, an agency contract was considered an "unclassified" juridic form, meaning under Portuguese law that the norms regulating such a relationship had to be sought by analogy with other sections of the Civil Code. This was most unsatisfactory and generated considerable litigation. The preamble to the law makes it clear that "... the recent ingress of Portugal into the European Economic Community" made it urgent and imperative that the legislator should intervene to counter the then existing legal ambiguities. The area which gave rise to frequent litigation was damages claimed by the agent when his contract was terminated. The Decree Law in question, as we shall see after a preliminary survey of the law, addresses this problem specifically.

As defined by Decree Law 178, "Agency is the contract by which one of the parties, autonomous, with a stable presence and for payment, obligates himself to promote for the account of another the conclusion of contracts in a certain geographical area or within a fixed circle of customers". As the agent is not an employee, he is not regulated by the local labour laws. He speaks for and is a legal presence of his distant principal. He is not a distributor as he does not hold large stocks or have obligations to purchase. Nor does he take financial risks or commitments with the hope of selling the product in the future. His authority is limited. The agent is the first step, a minimum effort by the principal (but normally involving maximum efforts by the agent) to penetrate a market without any significant investment. Basically, the agent is a prospector, searching out clients, marketing the product and, if permitted, signing contracts in the name of his principal after commercial terms are settled and approved by the principal.

Article 4 of the amended Decree Law confers to an agent the right to exclusivity provided this right is granted in a written document. The automatic application of an exclusivity clause does not run counter to the EEC competition standards since true agency agreements fall outside the ambit of Article 85(1). This is due to a Notice on Exclusive Dealing Contracts with Commercial Agents. In this respect there is a lacuna in the national law since there is no national law equivalent to this EEC Notice. Nevertheless, from the normally well-reasoned opinions emanating from the Portuguese Competition Council it can be expected that the local authorities will conclude by analogy that Portuguese agency agreements fall outside the Portuguese competition laws, which have been modelled scrupulously on the EEC laws.

The agent can nominate sub-agents unless the principal and the agent have agreed to the contrary, although this agreement is not required to be in writing, unlike the power of representation. Obviously, it is more prudent for such a limitation to be set out in a formal document. The agent is required to inform third parties of his powers (and hence his representation) by the posting of an announcement or sign at his office. This is a new development under Portuguese law.

Article 9 of Decree Law 178 allows the parties to agree, in writing, to a non-competition clause after the termination of the agreement for a maximum period of two years. Once again, there is no national law on whether or not two years violates *per se* the national anti-competition laws and further the law says "up to" meaning that each case is *sui generis.* Looking for guidance to the EEC jurisprudence, it is clear that any non-competition, after-contract prohibition should address the basic questions as to whether or not, in the particular case, the area is too wide, the restraint too long, or the trade has been unnecessarily restricted. The best counsel is to be moderate and not to impose draconian restrictions on a terminated agent.

Probably the most significant Article of Decree Law 178 for foreign investors will be Article 33(1) which is important enough to quote in full:

> "Without prejudice to any other right of indemnity which may exist pursuant to previous Articles, the agent has a right, after the termination of the contract, to damages in respect of customers so long as the following requirements are all satisfied:
>
> (a) the agent has brought new customers to the other party or has increased substantially the amount of business with the existing customers;
> (b) the other party has benefited substantially, after the termination of the contract, from the activity developed by the agent;
> (c) the agent has not received any payment for contracts negotiated or concluded, after the termination of the contract, from the customers referred to in (a)."

Article 34, as amended, has finally enacted an indemnity clause and thus put an end to much judicial uncertainty. This clause requires the indemnities of a terminated agent to be fixed in equitable terms but the indemnities cannot exceed an amount equal to the annual commissions received over the prior five years by the agent. Heretofore, the Portuguese courts have had to struggle to quantify the damages due to an indeterminate agency agreement but the latest amendments to the agency law has decisively put an end to this troublesome question.

Distribution Contracts

There is surely no more common commercial instrument than the distribution contract. In Portugal, there is no juridic regulation of national distribution contracts. Nor does EEC legislation affect domestic Portuguese distribution contracts, on the theory of the European Court of Justice that distribution contracts with a purely national character are not capable of affecting commerce between the Member States of the EEC. With no specific legislative guidance available to the foreign investor, there are only two suggestions which can be proferred to the potential investor as a guideline:

(a) Order 820/84 of 23rd October 1984 allows any interested party to solicit an opinion from the Competition Council as to the legality of a distribution contract in whole or in part.
(b) The Competition Council has also publicly stated (in its report of 1986) that the decisions of the European Court of Justice as well as Community legislation presuppose orientations which must be harmonised with the needs of

the national competition policy (in our case, Portugal) so as to promote legal certainty, the integration of markets and equality of treatment at both a national level and a Community level.

In the cases which have come before the Competition Council involving distribution contracts, clauses which have been held illegal have been those involving imposition of prices, absolute territorial protection, limitation of the distributor in the choice of his customers, imposition of a non-competition clause and an exclusive purchasing clause. However, inasmuch as Portugal has no specific legislation affecting distribution contracts, it continues to be relevant to view all such contracts in the light of the European Community legislation and in the case of any doubt to proceed under Order 820/84 for a declaration of legality.

Consortiums (Unincorporated Joint Ventures)

Quite often a foreign investor will associate himself with a local Portuguese company for a specific project in Portugal, the most common being in the area of construction. The parties normally intend that the foreign investor should bring expertise and probably funds and that the local partner will bring funds, labour and knowledge of the local market. Such ventures are normally not intended to be permanent and the usual form for such associations is the unincorporated joint venture, called in Portuguese the "contrato de consórcio", i.e. consortium. Regulation of the consortium is found in Decree Law 231/81 of 28th July 1981.

This Decree Law describes a specific form of joint venture which is really a contractual joint venture as distinguished from an equity joint venture. Equity joint ventures are so designated because they require the formation of a company with capital, or equity, a word often used to mean "capital". For there to exist capital, it must of course be contributed by partners and through the existence of partners has arisen the idea of a joint venture, meaning two or more entities collaborating. Our present concern is with the contractual joint venture although we shall examine in great detail in subsequent paragraphs the equity joint venture, particularly involving the foreign and a local investor. One aspect of Portuguese legal terminology should be emphasised. In Portugal, a company is thought of as a "social pact" between partners and capital in Portugal is referred to as "social capital".

Article 1 of the Decree Law defines the Portuguese notion of a consortium by stating it to be the realisation of a specific activity between two entities or by a contribution only from one party. It is not intended that one party only can make a contribution. For example, a foreign constructor could certainly contribute funds or personnel at a management level, e.g. chemical engineers in the design of an industrial plant. This notion of a consortium was given expression in a decree law to avoid forcing parties who wished to join together for the execution of an important public or private work from having to establish an entity such as a stock corporation or limited partnership. The purpose of the decree law is to encourage "partnerships" between entities on a simple basis.

To this end, the decree law allows the formation of a consortium by a simple contract in writing (Article 3) although if one of the contributions is to be land, e.g. the venture is between the owner of land and a builder, then a public deed would have to be executed before a public notary, since it is not possible in Portugal to convey land without such a public deed. A consortium has no legal existence. It cannot be sued in its own name. It is the individual members of the consortium who have to respond for whatever civil responsibility may exist because of their acts and one of these acts would be the signing of a contract with a third party. In a contract between an ostensible consortium and a third party, the signing member of the consortium is responsible; there is no automatic joint and several responsibility. It is possible for the contract of consortium to make all members of the consortium jointly liable. However this is not the consequence of the law but, as we shall see, of the terms of the consortium contract.

The decree law defines in detail how the rights and obligations between the parties are to be constituted; however, for purposes of foreign investment, probably the more important focus is on the types of consortium permitted under Portuguese law. This is divided into two types: internal and external consortia. The internal consortium takes place when neither party to the consortium indicates to third parties that such a contract exists. We can think of an internal consortium as being "vertical", where A, consortium member, furnishes goods to B, consortium member, who, without advising C, the customer, that B is acting as a member of a consortium, furnishes the goods or services. In this situation, the consortium is acting "vertically". Another type of internal consortium is "horizontal", where A and B each furnish goods or services to C, without mentioning that they are acting as members of a consortium. Each party contributes or furnishes his services to a third party in his individual name and capacity. The consortium's existence is not known. Not being known, the only party responsible to third parties is the consortium member acting directly with the third party, although the consortium contract may make all members jointly liable; this being so, there would of course be a right of recourse by one member against the other. Thus, should only B be sued, he could nevertheless seek A's share of the responsibility in a court action.

An external consortium exists when there is an express invocation of the consortium in the acts of the parties. But this express invocation does not alter the general rule of law that the consortium has no legal existence. In an external consortium it is permitted to use this expression in legal acts or on stationery or other forms of representation, it being sufficient to state "Consortium of ..." or "... in consortium".

This distinction between the two different types of consortia does not find expression in civil responsibility to third parties. While it might be thought an external consortium would obligate all members of the consortium to third parties, jointly and severally, in fact Article 19 expressly excludes this presumption, indicating that responsibility is casual and that the member at fault is the member who is responsible. Solidarity between the members is not to be presumed. From this, it can be concluded that the only advantage of an external consortium is the disadvantage of the secrecy of an internal consortium. Defective marble furnished by a secret member of an internal vertical consortium to the member dealing with third parties means that in any subsequent action brought by the third party, the origin of the responsibility is not easily known, an inconvenience surely for the third party dealing member of the consortium. Unless, therefore, there are political commercial reasons for an internal consortium, an external consortium would seem the more appropriate form for the foreign investor since the utilisation of the expression "Consortium of ..." will lead third parties to ask more questions and on their own initiative seek out responsibility or co-responsibility should it exist. This line of thought is further strengthened by Article 20 of the decree law which expressly prohibits the establishment of common funds by the consortium, this latter requirement being intended to make it clear that an unincorporated joint venture has no share capital nor independent legal existence. Each member of the unincorporated joint venture must be prepared to be responsible for his acts and respond with his assets.

To conclude, the formation of an external consortium in Portugal will have to be accompanied by a detailed contract between the parties so that the rights and obligations of all members of the consortium are fully established. Joint and several responsibility can only come as a result of the contract. For those foreign investors who do not wish to give publicity to their participation in any joint venture, the internal consortium will be the more appropriate vehicle.

Regulation of Foreign Investment

The international businessman or international lawyer, when doing business abroad, will naturally ask himself whether his investment is likely to be hampered by a multiplicity of licence requirements and controls. The answer in Portugal is that any foreign investment will probably be subject to fewer controls than it would be in the USA or England, with the added advantage that in a small country the centres of decision-making are all within easy reach of the investor and his lawyer.

Investment controls in Portugal underwent many changes between 1977, when the Foreign Investment Institute was formed, and 1989, when it was abolished. In 1989 the supervision of foreign investment was given to ICEP (Instituto do Comercio Externo de Portugal) and to the Bank of Portugal. It is anticipated that in 1992 ICEP will merge with the Portuguese Institute of Tourism and thereafter the new organism will be entitled the Institute of Portuguese External Relations (IREP). They now preside over a very liberal policy of foreign investment, requiring prior notification to the authorities, followed by the granting of a licence.

To understand foreign investment control in Portugal it is necessary to understand in practical terms how companies are formed in Portugal. The investor wishing to establish a stock corporation or a limited partnership does not, as he does in the USA or England, simply ask his lawyer to draft the articles and file them in the appropriate registry. In Portugal the formation of companies can only be carried out by a public notary, who is normally a lawyer who has chosen a public career working for the Ministry of Justice. His duty is to ensure that all parties to a transaction obey and comply with the law and, so far as possible, verify that the parties understand the consequences of their acts.

For example, if a developer buys a tract of land from a farmer, the purchase can only be effected by a public deed before the notary. Very often the notary will ask the seller if he has in fact received his money; he will ensure that the wife has consented if they are married and have jointly owned property; he will insist that the purchaser produces the necessary licences from the authorities consenting to the purchase. In similar fashion, the formation of a company requires the articles to be written by the public notary in his deed book (since the formation is regarded as a deed) and the notary will verify that the objects and the articles are in conformity with the law. Finally, if there is foreign capital involved, he will request the production of the necessary licence, whose terms will be recorded in an annex or appendix to the deed for future consultation. Thereafter the deed, when signed by all parties (including the notary), is filed with the relevant registry and published in the appropriate newspaper so that third parties are notified of the coming into existence of the company.

Under present legislation, the licence for the specific foreign investment is obtained from ICEP (Instituto do Comercio Externo de Portugal) which, in conjunction with the Bank of Portugal, implements the applicable regulations.

The existing laws, in chronological order, may be listed as follows:

- Decree Law 326/85 of 7th August 1985 regulating the import and export of capital between residents of the Member States of the EEC;
- Decree Law 351-C/85 of 26th August 1985 regulating operations relating to current invisibles between residents and non-residents;
- Normative Order 93/85 of 27th September 1985 subjecting commission contracts to licensing control by the Bank of Portugal;
- Normative Orders 98/85 of 17th October 1985 and 95/86 of 20th October 1986 subjecting technology contracts to control by the Bank of Portugal;
- Decree Law 38/86 of 4th March 1986 concerning the acquisition of rural property by non-residents;
- Decree Law 197-D/86 of 18th July 1986 adapting Portuguese legislation to the requirements of the European Economic Community;
- Regulatory Decree 24/86 of 18th July 1986 regulating the contractual system of investment in Portugal reserved for major investments of special interest and warranting the grant of fiscal incentives;
- Decree Law 214/86 of 2nd August 1986 defining the sectors open to foreign investment.

English translations of all these laws are available in a version promulgated by ICEP. In practice it is Decree Law 197-D which is generally applied to the average investment and it will be helpful to review some of its main aspects.

In the preface to the law it is stated that the "... Government felt that the time had now come to set up a new legal mechanism to handle incoming foreign investment and to supervise its implementation in clear, flexible terms". Consequently, there is introduced a "... system of prior declaration, where the competent authority will, by its silence (absence of objection), restrict itself to approval of the feasibility of investment projects submitted to it".

In practice this means that the foreign investor is asked to fill in a form headed "Prior Declaration of Foreign Investment". This basically calls for sufficient information to identify all relevant aspects of the investment, e.g. partners, capital, purpose, assets, projected expenses and income. It is essentially a form designed to ensure that an investment makes basic commercial sense.

When it is duly completed, this form is delivered to ICEP. Article 6 of the law gives the competent authorities two months to issue a final decision, in the absence of which the investor has the right to proceed with his investment. In practice, and due to the involvement of the public notary in the constitution of a company, no foreign investor would wish to rely on silence as signifying consent.

On the other hand, the declared purpose set out in the preface that the "... accession of Portugal to the European Community has also created the need to adjust regulations concerning foreign investment to conform with the new legal system ..." is effectively realised in the ready cooperation of ICEP in assisting the foreign investor, a spirit of cooperation which has its roots within the previous Foreign Investment Institute. It would be unusual for ICEP not to respond within two months and any delays are invariably attributable to the fact that information requested has not been supplied.

The ordinary foreign investor thinks of a foreign investment in terms of an import of capital. But this is not so. The law approaches the problem from a more practical base. Article 2 states that foreign investment operations are acts which give rise to "stable and long-lasting economic links from which effective decision-making power is obtained or strengthened, either directly or indirectly, immediately or cumulatively ..." when practised by non-residents or by local Portuguese companies which are regarded as subsidiaries of non-residents.

Admittedly there is a degree of vagueness in the language of the law, but the intent is clear: to regulate economic power as it is practised in a modern-day economy.

Article 3 indicates the acts and contracts which are subject to the law of prior declaration, even if not associated with the import of capital:

- establishment or expansion of branches or other forms of representation;
- total or partial acquisition of companies already in existence;
- participation and acquisition of holdings in the capital of companies;
- joint venture agreements;
- take-over of commercial or industrial establishments;
- take-over of agricultural businesses;
- construction;
- loans.

Although the present control of foreign investment in Portugal may be classified as a "prior notification" system, there are two important exceptions with practical implications for the foreign investor. Article 5 of Decree law 197-D allows a foreign investment to be made without prior notification if:

- the investment does not exceed 20% of the capital of the relevant company, provided there are no other means by which economic control could be exercised; or
- the investment involves transfers of holdings or other legal rights in national companies between non-resident members of the EEC.

These exceptions nevertheless require that the authorities be notified and further that any change of ownership be registered at the relevant commercial registry. In transactions involving the purchase of shares of a stock corporation the application of this exception presents no practical problem. There is a stock exchange catering for the transfer of shares in publicly traded companies, while for the privately controlled stock corporation, share transfer follows the well-understood method of endorsement of shares and delivery to the purchaser, followed by registration in the books of the company.

For companies which do not have a stock corporation structure, for example the private limited liability company or "sociedade por quotas" (referred to in Portugal as a "limitada" and often referred to by foreign investors as a "quota company") ownership is merely evidenced by a deed effected before the notary, in which the amount of the quota held by each partner is quantified. Consequently, there are practical problems in spite of the simplicity sought by the law.

In a quota company, there is no physical possession of any document of title which can be transferred from one party to another. Endorsement or delivery of a quota is impossible, since it is an intangible right created by a deed which is subsequently recorded at a commercial registry. The only way in Portugal to transfer ownership in a quota and to give notice to third parties is to execute a public deed before a public notary.

Transfers between non-resident EEC parties are therefore difficult to implement in Portugal. And yet this type of company is the overwhelmingly prevalent form of legal entity in Portugal due to its simple legal structure when compared to a stock corporation. It is the form of company the foreign investor is most likely to encounter in a merger or takeover or joint venture. How then can a transfer between non-residents, effected outside Portugal, perhaps by a contract of bill of sale, be legally implemented in Portugal?

Although there may be theoretical solutions to this problem, the simplest and most practical advice for a foreign investor, even if he is not technically required to do so, is to notify ICEP, obtain a licence (which is easily obtained) and proceed to a transfer of quotas before the notary, followed by registration at the commercial registry.

In theory, foreign investment involving EEC members receives preferential treatment and can only be rejected under specific circumstances detailed in article 7(2). Again, in theory, article 8, regulating foreign investment by non-EEC investors, requires ICEP to examine the investment project in the light of its effect on the economy of Portugal. In theory, EEC investors receive preferential treatment.

In practice, ICEP makes no distinction between EEC and non-EEC investors, processing all applications in a prompt fashion. No doubt especially large projects submitted by a non-EEC investor would require assessment in accordance with article 8 and much information would be requested. But then it is precisely the large investments that are the most sought-after, so that bureaucratic obstacles are least probable in such cases.

Of particular interest for large investments is Regulatory Decree 24/86 which empowers the Portuguese government to execute "foreign investment contracts" with a foreign investor. The purpose of this regulatory decree is to permit the government to grant fiscal benefits and incentives to foreign investors in exchange for the conpletion of an agreed project in accordance with agreed objectives and within agreed periods.

The regulatory decree is derived from a former law which established what was then known as an "administrative contract". Although the decree is little more than a general statement of principles, the foreign investment contract affords great flexibility to the foreign investor and its application should be sought wherever appropriate.

Naturally, the question most frequently asked by the foreign investor is whether he can freely transfer his profits abroad or even the entire investment in the event of a sale or dissolution and liquidation. The law clearly allows this and, what is more important, the writer can confirm that more than two decades of experience with the Bank of Portugal, even during the times of foreign reserve shortages created by political changes during 1974 has demonstrated the commitment of the Bank of Portugal to protecting the foreign investor to the full extent of the law.

Article 9 of Decree Law 197-D makes it quite clear that what the average businessman considers his investment and profit can be exported.

Some specific types of investment deserve special mention, the most prominent being investments in land, such as tourist enterprises or large agricultural developments. Due to the growing importance of the tourist industry in Portugal, this sector of private investment has exploded. Unfortunately, it is also the one area where many legal problems occur.

Normally a tourist investment begins with the purchase of land and the purchase of land in Portugal comes within the terms of Decree Law 38/86. The printed word of this decree law appears simple enough: individuals not residing in Portugal will be permitted to purchase rural land not exceeding 5000 square metres. However, the decree law refers to "rural property" and 1000 square metres of land in downtown Lisbon, is not rural land. It is urban land. Many foreign investors believe that if they purchase less than 5000 square metres they have complete freedom of investment. But this is not the case.

Besides the limit of 5000 square metres, the law also states that the purchase must be destined for the construction of a home. The purchase of real estate frequently seems to generate problems for the investor. And yet observation of a few simple guidelines will ensure a proper purchase and sale of a hotel or other real estate investment.

The investor finding a hotel site should first sign a contract subject to approval by the authorities of his investment as well as the use of the land. Approval of a tourist development will take time and involve many different authorities. Secondly, knowing that much time is needed for approval, the investor can submit a summarised description of the project to the authorities so that the land can be bought within a reasonable period of time. Preliminary approvals do not take that long. Additionally, there are many investment projects for sale which have already been approved by the authorities. However alterations, while permitted in theory, are not automatic. The foreign investor wishing to purchase a hotel project already approved on paper should still take the necessary contractual safeguards. Fourthly, purchasing agricultural land in Portugal for the purposes of large-scale fruit or vegetable farming can become a legal nightmare if proper title searches are not made.

It is almost the universal practice in Portugal to describe land as "bounded by Mr White on the north and Mr Black on the south and Mr Green on the east and Mr Red on the west". What does that tell lawyers? Absolutely nothing. The purchase of agricultural land will involve speaking to neighbours, defining the boundaries in advance, putting up boundary markers, arranging for a survey to be drawn and attaching it both to the contract and then to the final deed before the notary. In most countries with a strong peasant tradition, land and its boundaries are very sacred and parties will go to court over ten metres.

Although non-EEC investors are subject in theory to different legal rules, there is in practice no difference in treatment and under the present liberalised EEC practice of encouraging free movement of capital, Portugal processes the overwhelming majority of applications for foreign investment as if they were covered by Decree Law 326/85. It would have to be an investment with very unusual characteristics to warrant prolonged scrutiny by ICEP or the Bank of Portugal.

Price Control

Any consideration of a foreign investment in Portugal must surely take into account the present structure of price controls insofar as it affects the product or service to be launched. As a preliminary synopsis, it can be stated, in the words of the Competition and Price Control Board (not to be confused with the Competition Council which has supervisory and appeal powers over the Board) that "... Step by step, the policy of price control is giving way to competition policy ... On the other hand the control of inflation is being sought more and more by recourse to budget, monetary, exchange rate and income policies". Price control does exist in Portugal but the product list is continually being reduced and is confined to those products or services with six digits in the CAE classification. This CAE classification means Classification of Economic Activities published by the National Institute of Statistics, known as INE in Portugal, which is located at Av. Antonio José de Almeida, 1078 Lisbon, Portugal. Furthermore, price control in Portugal does not necessarily mean formula-setting prices. It can also mean "watched", i.e. the Price Control Board has the right to intervene in the setting of the price if it feels the price has become speculative. For example, synthetic detergents used commonly in homes are subject to this price regime of "vigiados" or "being watched".

Portugal has a long history of "cooperativism", meaning that much of the economic history of Portugal in the period following the Second World War was dominated by associations of industrialists who, in close collaboration with the Government, established prices for sensitive goods and effectively kept out competition. On the one hand, the Government secured social peace by carefully controlling prices of bread and other essential items. On the other hand an oligarchy of entrepreneurs easily dominated vital industries, including textiles, petroleum and ship building to name but a few. When the 1974 Revolution destroyed this social pact, starting in 1974 and culminating in 1984, Portugal went through various stages of price control, gradually evolving towards a modern economy.

The present system of price control in Portugal, whose jurisdiction is confined to the Board of Competition and Price Control, involves a number of categories, as follows:

(a) maximum prices;
(b) declared prices;
(c) contracted prices;
(d) fixed margins;
(e) watched prices;
(f) free prices.

Only two categories are probably not self-evident. For those goods indicated by the Secretary of State for Internal Commerce as being subject to a "declared prices" regime, which is made by reference to the appropriate CAE six-digit number, there is a qualifying threshold. From 1st January 1992, a company with total gross revenues of 825,000,000 escudos and revenues of 165,000,000 escudos for the particular product or service subject to this regime had to notify the Price Control Board of their practised prices and changes thereto when made. The prices, unless contested by the Price Control Board, remained valid. The other category which is not self-evident is that of "free prices". This is a misnomer, as it was intended to indicate goods or services formerly (but no longer) subject to control.

The effect of the various existing regimes can be summarised as follows:

- the regime of "maximum prices" indicates maximum

prices declared by the Government for a particular service or product;

- "declared prices" require the company on its own initiative to send in the prices it will practise, with accompanying material of an accounting nature. The Price Control Board has 60 days to contest the quantification if it is not in agreement;
- "contracted prices" are prices agreed upon between the company and the Government and normally relate to prices for extremely sensitive products, such as electricity;
- prices with "fixed margins" mean prices where the Government, instead of directly setting the price, analyses the cost structure and then sets a limit to the profit margin;
- watched prices mean that the Government follows and watches the evolution of the product in question;
- "free prices" are simply those prices for goods or services which are no longer subject to price control.

From the above discussion it might be assumed that prices on most products and services in Portugal are subject to control. This is not true. In fact, reviewing the list of products and services subject to a form of price control reveals a rather short, narrow list. Price control does not constitute any barrier to investment in Portugal. As a random illustration, on 1st January 1992, the following goods or services were determined by the Secretary of State for Commerce as being affected by one or another price control regime (all necessitating a CAE classification of six digits):

- declared price: precious metals (CAE 2302.8.0);
- watched price: sea salt (CAE 2903.1.0);
- free price: frozen fish (CAE 3114.2.0);
- fixed margin: refined sugar (3118.2.0);
- contracted price: school books (CAE 3420.2.2);
- maximum price: tobacco (CAE 3140.0.0).

Competition Law

Prior to the enactment of legislation specifically designed to regulate competition (which only took place in Portugal in 1983), the primary source of competition law was to be found in the Code of Industrial Property, Article 212. This was enacted in 1940 and remains in force. In particular, Article 212 defines unlawful competition as being "... every act of competition contrary to the norms and honest uses of any branch of economic activity. The following are expressly prohibited ...". There then follows a lengthy enumeration, but not intended to be exhaustive, which includes acts creating confusion between establishments, false claims as to the quality of products, unauthorised references intended to benefit a name or product, false advertising, false indications of origin (or its suppression), illicit appropriation of trade secrets or their disclosure. The fact that Article 212 is to be found in the Industrial Property Code does not confine its application to trade marks or patents. It is intended to prevent unfair competition in general, but its limited use had no doubt been due to its constituting part of the Industrial Property Code. Yet the law in theory has broad implications and many applications.

The law is intended to prohibit conduct contrary to the norms of "honest" customs (in English we might say "good or time-honoured customs"). On 30th May 1957, the Attorney General of Portugal defined the objective of Article 212 in these words:

> "Illegal competition is constituted by those acts repudiated by the normal conscience of merchants and contrary to the honest uses of commerce which are capable of causing prejudice to the company of a competitor by the usurpation, even if partial, of his clients."

With such a definition, we might ask if any form of competitive behaviour is permitted in Portugal. But of course, as indicated in subsequent sections, more recent laws, by specifically regulating anti-competitive acts, implicitly recognise that competitive behaviour must indeed exist and be permitted. Nevertheless, in this age of aggressive marketing, it will be helpful to call attention to what Article 212 specifically enjoins:

- false statements intended to discredit a competitor (this does not prevent comparative advertising, but only false comparisons);
- advertising which contains false claims about the quality or characteristics of products;
- confusion between products or services.

Article 212 is a general but highly useful provision for those unusual fact situations which the imaginative lawyer is often called upon to analyse.

The law regulating anti-competitive behaviour and concentration between companies in Portugal is set out in two distinct decree laws, which are discussed under the appropriate headings below.

EEC Merger Control

Portugal now has two systems of merger control: community law regulation as set out in Regulation 4064/89 and its own national merger control. The EEC Regulation, to be applicable, must involve a transaction with a "community dimension". That is to say the parties concerned must have an aggregate worldwide turnover of at least 5000m ECU and a community-wide turnover of at least 250m ECU. These thresholds are unlikely to be reached by the average investor in Portugal. On the other hand, a merger or acquisition in Portugal which results in control of more than 20% of the relevant market, or which results in local sales exceeding approximately US$35m, or which results in a substantial alteration in the competitive structure of the relevant market requires pre-notification to the merger authorities. In view of the low monetary and percentage thresholds, it is essential to consider in detail local Portuguese merger control.

Just as merger control under Community law has its historical roots in Articles 85 and 86 of the Treaty of Rome, so Portugal's merger control has its roots in earlier national legislation enacted prior to the EEC Merger Regulation and also modelled on Articles 85 and 86 of the Treaty of Rome. Indeed merger and acquisition law cannot, as a practical matter, realistically be separated from the control of general competitive behaviour, which in Portugal is regulated by Decree Law 422/83 of 3rd December 1983.

Portuguese Competition Law

In the preamble to Decree Law 422 it is stated that the defence "... of competition constitutes, in truth, one of the essential tools of economic policy". Investors familiar with Articles 85 and 86 of the Treaty of Rome will have no trouble in understanding what is con- sidered to be anti-competitive behaviour. Combining various articles from Decree Law 422, we can list in schematic form practices regarded as restrictive to competition before there is any merger:

- the imposition of minimum prices and the application of discriminatory prices or selling conditions, most frequently occurring in distribution contracts;
- refusal to sell goods or render services. This frequently occurs when a well-known brand is imported by a parallel importer, who must then confront the chagrin of the authorised distributor who thought his product was protected from competition;
- agreements whatever their form, between companies which restrict competition.

Here, we must pause in our analysis, for while Decree Law 422 does not have as its object the regulation of mergers there is no doubt that mergers are frequently restrictive of competition and this law has no percentage thresholds. Decree Law 422 does not establish pre-notification procedures, unlike the official merger control. Rather, it leaves the Competition Council to investigate any violations of this law. In other words, a merger falling short of the threshold of the merger control law may nevertheless be reviewed by the Competition Council under Decree Law 422. Furthermore, article 15 of Decree Law 422 grants a right to any party to request certification from the Competition Council that the provisions of the Decree Law have not been violated.

The particular practices, whether or not resulting from a merger, which are likely to be considered anti-competitive, are specifically those which:

- directly or indirectly fix or recommend buying or selling prices;
- limit or control production, distribution, technical development or investment;
- divide markets or sources of supply;
- apply, whether systematically or occasionally, discriminatory price conditions;
- involve direct or indirect refusal to buy or sell goods or render services;
- subordinate the execution of contracts to the acceptance of supplementary obligations which are not reasonably related to the subject of the contract;
- are considered anti-competitive under international conventions to which Portugal is a party;
- involve abuses exercised by one or more companies occupying a dominant position. Here the law is somewhat more demanding, requiring at least a 30% share of the market to constitute dominance where two companies are involved; 50% for three companies; 65% for more than three companies. The reason for the reference to one or more companies and to these different percentages can

> be found in article 14(4) which states: For the purposes of application of this article, the word 'company' is intended to mean a group of companies which, although legally separate, act in concert in the market by virtue of interdependence or subordination of a financial, contractual, managerial or other nature."

The investor familiar with Articles 85 and 86 of the Treaty of Rome will know that implementation of these articles has not hindered the commercial development of the EEC and that the application of these articles is subject to the *de minimus* requirement that the effects of the anti-competitive behaviour must have practical consequences. Additionally, commercial common sense avoids the majority of the prohibitions. There is no need to set minimum selling prices if the manufacturer adheres to fixed wholesale prices. Distributors know how to calculate margins. Division of markets should never be created by contract, which would constitute a *per se* violation of the law. Markets naturally tend to partition themselves through efficient after-sales service. Cartels and gentlemen's agreements not to compete are no longer seriously considered by the international businessman. Sufficient for one leader in an industry to raise or lower prices for all the others to be likely to do the same. The European Court of Justice has said many times that similar behaviour by competitors does not necessarily indicate collusive behaviour.

From a legal point of view the abuse of dominant position provisions of Decree Law 422 are more troublesome but then with a minimum threshold of 30% the national merger law would apply in any event.

The Competition Council

Naturally the foreign investor may frequently feel that the maze and complexity of anti-competition laws act as a deterrent to mergers and acquisitions which have a sound commercial basis for taking place. It therefore helps to have a practical working knowledge of the actual business climate of any country, since legal theory and practical implementation of the law do not always converge.

In this respect, it is useful to understand the role of the Portuguese Competition Council as its views are important both in terms of anti-competition law and merger law. In its report of 1984/5 presented to the Ministry of Industry and Commerce, the Council stated:

> "One of the problems which has preoccupied the Council since the beginning was the system of control of restrictive commercial practices, specifically control of combinations (the Portuguese word used is "coligaçãos" which is imprecise and in common language literally means getting-together, i.e. joint ventures, mergers, collaborative arrangements etc) and abuses of dominant position."

In the same report, the Council encourages the practice of pre-notifying to the Council any contemplated legal association so that companies "... may solicit an opinion as to the legality, illegality or justification of any agreement, agreed practice, decision of an association of companies or abuse of dominant position".

Before examining the philosophy of the Competition Council it is helpful to understand its legal function. The Council was initially created by Decree Law 422/83 and charged with responsibility, pursuant to the terms of article 20, for (*inter alia*):

- deciding on processes relating to restrictions on competition;
- proposing to the relevant ministry directives for the application of Decree Law 422/83.

The function of the Competition Council is quasi-judicial. It is not an investigative body. The investigative body which can inquire into anti-competitive behaviour, analagous to the

Commission of the EEC, is the "Direccão-Geral de Concorrencia e Preços", which may be translated as "Competition and Prices Board". The latter is the group empowered to examine practices in the business community, and to act as a watchdog against anti-competitive behaviour.

However it is more important for the foreign investor to understand the philosophy of the Competition Council, since it is the Council which decides cases and which, under merger control law, resolves any process notified to the Ministry of Commerce if the Ministry has any doubts as to the validity of a proposed merger.

Additionally, Order 820/84 of 23rd October 1984 establishes procedures whereby a party in doubt as to the legality of any business practice can request from the Competition Council, a negative clearance or exemption from the application of Decree Law 422, a process referred to in the Council's 1984/5 report.

For the first time in 1987, upon an application presented by Quimigal, EP *et al.* in June 1985 for a declaration of legality, the Council was called upon to decide, under a procedure initiated by virtue of Order 820, whether or not Decree Law 422 would be applied to a horizontal cooperation between companies in the area of production and distribution involving the establishment of common affiliates. In summary, this related to a form of cooperation by which three companies agreed to process raw materials acquired by their common affiliate, and to carry out agreed plans of production, with each company then being obliged to deliver to their common affiliate the finished product for packaging and distribution under the distinctive trademark of the affiliate.

The Council clearly saw the restrictive features of the proposed constitution of a common affiliate and listed them succinctly, in its own language:

- "... almost absolute annulment of freedom of supply and sale conditions on the part of the associated companies and the affiliate ...";
- "... limitation and common planning of production and reduction of offer ...".

In a long and reasoned analysis supported by market detail the Council concluded that the proposed constitution of the affiliate should be permitted on grounds of promoting economic development and (for our purposes most significantly) the Council took the opportunity to announce its economic views concerning Portugal and the EEC: "... The Council gave special attention to the problem of companies having to improve their competitive performance because of the country joining the Common Market ... especially the competition economic agents faced from the international economy". Some conditions were imposed by the Council and the suspension of Decree Law 422 was provided only until 31st December 1991.

In 1988, the Competition Council in its annual report took the opportunity to clarify the relationship between community legislation in the area of competition law and national law. The council stated as follows: "The community law prevails over the national law. This means that if there is a conflict of legal principles, the solution given by community law will prevail". The Council went on to provide guidelines as to the inter-relationship of community law and national law in Portugal:

"(a) if the behaviour would be prohibited by community law and permitted by national law, the prohibition prevails;
(b) if the behaviour would not be prohibited by community law but would be forbidden by national law, the prohibition would prevail;
(c) if the behaviour would benefit from an exemption from

the Commission (i.e. would be prohibited but justified), the community exemption will prevail;

(d) if the behaviour is covered by a specific category of block exemption under a Regulation, the application of national law cannot prejudice the effect of such exemption".

Furthermore, the Competition Council has stated in its official 1986 report that the Competition Council is a "jurisdiction" in the sense that this term is used for purposes of interpretation of Article 177 of the Treaty of Rome. Thus the Competition Council has the right to petition the European Court of Justice as to the application of any community law or regulation in Portugal and as to possible conflicts with national competition law.

However the role of the Competition Council extends also to mergers and acquisitions.

Concentration Control and the Competition Council

The fundamental law regulating mergers and acquisitions in Portugal is Decree Law 428/88 of 19th November 1988 which was enacted prior to EEC Regulation 4064/89 of 21st December 1989 concerning the "Control of Concentration between Undertakings". As in the EEC Regulation, Decree Law 428 controls "concentrations", a word in Portuguese which covers mergers and acquisitions but also other legal situations as we shall see below.

Decree Law 428 states in its preamble that the text in question is closely related to the preparatory EEC studies concerning mergers. In schematic form, Decree Law 428 is applicable to a merger or acquisition when:

(a) the volume of sales resulting from the concentration is equal to or superior to 5 billion escudos, or;

(b) the share of the market for the relevant product or group of like products is equal to or superior to 20% of the Portuguese market or 5% of the community market; or
(c) the result of the concentration alters substantially the competitive structure of the market for the goods or services in question without any exceptions of the type envisaged by Decree Law 422 being apparent. Banks and insurance companies are exempt from the application of this generic principle as well as a special group of companies defined by the "Code of Portuguese Commercial Societies" as companies constituting a group and which are undergoing a reorganisation. This refers to a group of companies which are already forming a concentration which is specifically encouraged by the law such that it would be senseless to penalise them.

But what is a "concentration" under Portuguese law? Article 2 of Decree Law 428 defines a concentration as resulting from a merger or decapitalisation of two or more companies—our traditional merger—but it also includes the situation where a singular or collective entity obtains "decisive influence" over another company. In Portuguese, the word used is "determinante" which means "sufficient to determine" and which for legal purposes is more easily understood as meaning decisive. Additionally, although the legislation speaks of decisive influence over another "empresa", i.e. company, a person is surely also an "empresa" as we cannot expect the legislators to have intended that the constellation of rights and duties created by a corporate entity should be different from those of an individual person.

By virtue of Article 2, and bearing in mind the diverse legal mechanisms by which companies can create legal relations, from simple contractual rights to mergers, it is necessary to know what Portuguese law regards as decisive influence. Article 3 of Decree Law 424 lays down a number of guidelines. Decisive influence will be deemed to exist:

(a) between companies when there is created a group relationship or domination (a subject we shall examine in further detail in our discussion of the various permitted business forms in Portugal); or
(b) where an individual person or corporate entity acquires from another "society" at least 10% of its assets; or
(c) where an individual person or corporate entity acquires a participation in the capital of another "society" exceeding 10%, with a right to vote and, by means of the articles of association or a private agreement, the purchaser is able to take or block decisions at a meeting of the shareholders or of any of the "organs" of the seller; or, by means of contracts between "societies", is able to determine or block its commercial or investment policies, the utilisation of technology or raw materials or the distribution of products.

In the three subdivisions listed above, the Portuguese legislation refers in each case to "sociedade". Whether the legislator meant to confine the application of the law to "companies" and not "persons" must await judicial clarification. Inasmuch as the Decree Law is only applicable when sales of at least 5 billion escudos are involved, cases involving individual sellers will be rare, although it continues to be a theoretical lacuna in the law.

From a practical viewpoint, the two thresholds of either 5 billion escudos or 20% of the Portuguese market substantially restrict the application of the law. Nevertheless, particularly in transactions involving multi-national companies, or companies with pan-European operations, the provision affecting "concentrations which substantially alter the competitive structure of the market" is not very precise. Unfortunately, as stated in its 1989 report, no process involving Decree Law 428 had, as at the date of that report, been submitted to the Competition Council for consideration.

Notification Procedures

Consistent with its declared purpose of harmonising Portuguese law with EEC law, the Decree Law contains provisions for prior notification to the government in the case of "concentrations".

A pre-notification is mandatory whenever the law is applicable. However, lawyers are bound to utilise the procedure even in cases where the application of the law is not so clear. The notification is made to the Ministry of Commerce and Tourism which has two government bodies to assist it. It can request the Council on Competition and Prices to conduct further investigations (presumably so as to enable it to fully understand the facts) or it can also refer the question for consideration by the Competition Council. Naturally, if the Ministry believes there is no infringement of the Decree Law, it can decide to do nothing. The lack of a response from the Ministry within the time periods established by law is deemed to mean "no opposition to the realisation of the projected concentration".

Article 4 of Decree Law 428 indicates when it is mandatory to refer the proceedings to the Competition Council. This will occur when any one of the following eventualities arises from the concentration:

(a) a reduction in the number or range of suppliers or consumers;
(b) the creation of conditions conducive to a situation of monopoly or quasi-monopoly;
(c) prejudice to consumers' choice in terms of materials, prices or other sources of supply;
(d) a major reduction or elimination of competition, particularly the elimination of distribution networks;
(e) distortion of price structures by discriminatory or abusive pricing;
(f) breach of the rules of competition of the EEC or

Portugal.

Decree Law 428 does not by its terms indicate the form or contents of the pre-notification. Nevertheless, from practical experience and interviews with the Ministry, a pre-notification to the Ministry can be made by either party to the transaction and in relation to the purchaser, the seller and other parties involved (perhaps local subsidiaries) there must be indicated:

- their corporate names;
- the amount of capital to be issued, which may be different from the capital actually issued;
- their legal headquarters;
- the principal product lines;
- an economic analysis of the relevant market, market shares, and whether the purchase will affect competition in the relevant market;
- reasons for the purchase;
- how the purchase will be implemented;
- the Portuguese tax reference of each party, if applicable;
- their registration numbers at the Commercial Registry if applicable.

There are no special forms to complete and the notification can be made by a comprehensive presentation in writing addressed to the Ministry beginning:
"Your Excellency:
Pursuant to Decree Law 428 etc.".

Law of Commercial Societies

Sources of Information

Information about an existing commercial company in Portugal can be garnered from consulting the records of the commercial conservatory which exists in every major city (e.g.

Lisbon, Porto, Coimbra, Leiria) and for the rare consultation of a company located in a rural area an inquiry at the local town hall will be sufficient to discover where to find the conservatory for that particular locality. In other words, every company in Portugal is registered at some commercial conservatory. The records of the conservatory are the life and death of a company and reveal its complete history since its inception: capital on formation, partners, articles of incorporation, division of capital, transfers perhaps made through the years, augments of capital and dissolution if such should be the case. A careful perusal of the records reveals everything that has transpired legally.

Fortunately for the foreign investor, the law of commercial societies was completely rewritten and codified and on 1st November 1986 the Code of Commercial Societies (subsequently designated as the CCS) entered into full force and effect. One of the innovations the CCS brought about was to require the annual acounts and report of the management for all companies, except general partnerships, to be registered at the commercial conservatory. Beyond the normal accounting material, the CCS requires that the report and accounts reveal any transactions which have taken place between the company and its management; the purchase of its own shares and the reason for same; a projection of the future evolution of the company and a proposal of the application of the annual financial result.

Other reliable sources of information in Portugal are the banks. In a small country, company profiles are quickly created. There also exist reliable organisations which will do a credit check on a company. Such credit checks will reveal any actions brought against a particular company. There are no central records kept of court procedures and some of the credit agencies and banks actually send every day to the court house a functionary to look at the actions which are posted on the bulletin board.

There also exists the possibility of gaining information by going to the offices of the *Imprensa Nacional* (literally govenment press). Every company at formation must publish its articles and they must be published in the govenment gazette as well as a newspaper with good circulation. The *Imprensa Nacional* has organised records and an interested party can easily locate preliminary information such as corporate headquarters, which will then indicate what is the relevant commercial conservatory. The *Imprensa Nacional* will have much of the information recorded at the commercial conservatory about the legal history of the company, although not all information is published, e.g. management changes, composition of board of directors.

Whether purchasing an interest in a company, or forming a Portuguese subsidiary, the foreign investor will require a general knowledge of the basics of the various types of companies in Portugal, their similarities and differences.

The subsequent sections deal with the more commonly known legal forms regulated by Portuguese law, specifically in the CCS.

General partnership

The general partnership in Portugal is denominated "Sociedade em Nome Colectivo". In a Portuguese partnership, the following rules are applicable:

- the partners are responsible secondarily but jointly and severally for the debts of the company;
- a partner assumes upon admittance to the partnership the debts of the partnership;
- the partnership articles must specify the capital, the form of the contribution and the percentages of each partner;
- the partnership name either contains all the names of the partners or some and ends with "& Company";
- partners cannot compete with the general partnership;

- a partnership interest can only be transfered with the consent of all the other partners;
- a partnership interest is not subject to execution, only his right to profit;
- upon the death of a partner, the partnership is not automatically dissolved. It may pay the estate and continue; or the successor in interest may enter into the partnership if all are in agreement: or the partnership can be dissolved.

The law allows a partner to be able to demand his "pay-out" under certain circumstances, one of which includes the completion of ten years as a partner in a general partnership whose articles of partnership do not foresee any termination date. Unless the partnership articles provide to the contrary, each partner has the right to one vote. Unless the articles establish another rule, the partnership articles can only be changed by unanimous vote but in any event the alteration permitted by law is very restricted. The articles can only lower the requirement of 100% to 75%.

In summary, a general partnership under Portuguese law requires an awareness of some of the above, perhaps unknown general principles, particularly those dealing with an obligatory pay-out and the alteration of the usual majority rule principle.

Limited Partnership

A limited partnership in Portuguese law is denominated "Sociedade em Comandita" and the law foresees two types of limited partnerships: with and without shares. A limited partnership differs essentially from a general partnership in that there has to be one or more general partners who are responsible without limitation for the debts of the company. However, sometimes venture capital is needed by promoters and this can be achieved by admitting partners whose responsibility to creditors is limited to their contribution. Consequently, the expression: limited partnership. Some general principles can be synthesised:

- a limited partnership by shares requires a minimum of five limited partners;
- the name of the firm must contain the name of at least one of the general partners and the Portuguese equivalent of "Limited Partnership" or "Limited Partnership with Shares";
- in a limited partnership without shares the transfer of interest of a generl partner is only possible if all the other general partners agree;
- transfer of interest of a limited partner is subject to the rules applicable to quota companies and hence, unless there was a prohibition in the articles of the limited partnership, this is easily accomplished.
- regarding a limited partnership by shares, the transfer of shares is subject to those rules applicable to stock corporations and, once again, the articles of the partnership can govern such a transfer; otherwise, any transfer is free of pre-conditions.

Inter-company Relationships: Group or Affiliated Companies

In recognition of the complex relationships affecting modern corporations, the newly enacted Portuguese Code of Commercial Companies (Codigo Sociedades Comerciais) (CSC) (1986) codified the rules affecting "inter-company relationships". This assumes particular importance in view of Decree Law 428 which includes within the definition of a "concentration" situations whereby one company gains decisive influence over another. Article 2 of Decree Law 428 defines a concentration to exist when "... between companies there shall be created a relationship of domination or of group ...". Companies in a group relationship or where there exists domination are given separate treatment in the Code of

Commercial Companies which seeks to regulate what we can think of as inter-company relationships. However, "inter-company relationships" are not the words used in the CSC. For those interested in comparative law, the expression used in Portuguese and in the relevant Code is "Sociedades Coligadas". We can translate the word "coligação", (from the verb "coligar" of which "coligadas" is the past participle) as meaning "an alliance, a confederation, a union". Transposing this idea into the law, we see that the concept intended is the formation of relationships by virtue of shares or voting rights, whether by contract or other means. Therefore the expression "company groups or affiliates" will be used here in a broad sense denoting the existence of some means of control. Consequently, by the expression inter-company relationships we mean a legal right conferring on one company a power over another company, the magnitude of which or the various powers in possession causing the situation to be regulated in the CSC.

Obviously, it is precisely within inter-company relationships involving various tiers of shareholding that a remote Luxembourg-based corporation can control a local subsidiary. We can imagine a situation where a Luxembourg company owns 51% of a Belgian company which in its turn owns 51% of a Portuguese company. It needs no analysis on our part to demonstrate how easily, through majority voting, Luxembourg controls Portugal without even appearing on the corporate records as a shareholder.

Article 481 of the Code of Commercial Companies defines "sociedades coligadas" to include four forms, to wit: (a) relationship of simple participation, (b) reciprocal relationship, (c) relationship of domination and (d) group relationship, which last classification is further subdivided into groups of "total domination", "common management" and "contractual dependency". Although only (c) and (d) are within the ambit of the merger law, all four forms warrant our attention as the existence of these forms confers obligations on the parties to make their ownership transparent by advising the other owners. These rules are only applicable to quota companies, share companies and limited partnerships. These are the only company forms subjected to the discipline of "sociedades coligadas", i.e. inter-company relationships".

The rules applicable to inter-company relationships only affect those companies with their headquarters in Portugal or foreign companies which dominate a Portuguese company. The concept of domination is discussed below.

The simplest form of inter-company relationship is that of simple participation. Simple participation exists when Company A owns at least 10% of Company B. If this relationship exists, Company A must therafter advise Company B of any further sales or acquisitions it makes of Company B's quotas or shares.

There is considered to be a relationship of reciprocal participation when Company A and Company B each own at least 10% of the quotas or shares of the other. Should this ownership interest exist, any further purchases or sales of the other's quotas or shares must be communicated; otherwise, voting rights are suspended.

Companies are in a relationship of domination when one company can exercise a dominating influence over another; this dominating influence exists when one company has a majority of capital of the other, or more the 50% of the voting rights or can designate more than 50% of the management. Once this relationship exists, the merger laws are also applicable. Additionally, the company dominated cannot acquire the shares or quotas of the company dominating it. Furthermore, if a foreign company is considered to be dominating a local Portuguese company, then this foreign company is liable to the company and its partners for any mismanagement.

Finally, there are those companies considered to be in a relationship of "group", which comprises three different types. The first is when one company is the only shareholder of another company. This is considered total domination. The consequences of total domination are far-reaching and are considered to exist with less then 100% ownership. Under the law of Portugal, the concept of total domination exists when a company acquires at least 90% of the capital of another company. Should total domination exist (90% or more), the dominating company can compel the sale of the balance of the shares or quotas and if it does not exercise this legally conferred option, the minority quota or share owners can compel the purchase of their interests. The values to be paid are those to be derived from the official accounts.

Relationship of Domination

The complexity of these provisions can be illustrated in relation to mergers and acquisitions. The writer can recall the merger of a major US producer of paint products outside Portugal with a competitor. It was agreed that the two local Portuguese subsidiaries of the two merging companies would not merge in Portugal in order to avoid excessive tax burdens. Nevertheless the managers of both subsidiaries were instructed to report to the European manager of the merged companies for purposes of administrative control. Although legally separate, the two Portuguese subsidiaries were clearly controlled by a third party because the power to hire and fire gives the power to manage and determine policy, and to manage and determine policy means to have dominant influence as businessmen understand that term. In the example cited there was no thought of collusive action, nor any attempt to circumvent Portuguese laws. But this was a case where, without a formal merger having taken place, a dominant influence was obtained, which theoretically would have required notice to the merger authorities assuming the relevant thresholds were exceeded.

Furthermore a company in Portugal which acquires a role of domination in another company may find itself liable for the pre-existing debt of the company it controls. Article 501 of the CSC makes the controlling company responsible for the debt of the controlled company and Article 491 when referring to "group constituted by total dominion" make this Article 501 applicable. A clear example: this writer can remember the case of the American company which ordered plastic moulds from a Portuguese manufacturer. The moulds were sent and found to be defective. At the same time, the mould manufacturer underwent a financial crisis and filed for protection from its creditors. During the proceedings, another mould manufacturer reached an agreement with creditors and purchased all the shares of the company in trouble. The American importer had no knowlege of these proceedings nor does it appear that the purchaser of the shares knew of the possibility of litigation. Eventually the American importer took steps to protect its rights and when the purchaser of shares was discovered, an action was brought against both the original manufacturer and the acquirer of all its shares, which was a financially sound company.

The above example illustrates a case of total dominion. But of course, very often foreign investors acquire only a controlling interest, perhaps a little more than half the votes. Does the foreign investor run the risk of the consequences pointed out above? Only if an acquisition of 90% or more is consummated. Less than 90%, for technical reasons, we can safely reassure the foreign investor: the acquisition of shares will not create liability. Above 90%, the prospective foreign investor would be well advised to conduct a thorough audit with detailed seller's warranties.

The second type of group companies is when two or more companies create a third company which shall be subject to common management. However, this can only be done with due regard for the rules on competition, i.e. this type of group concept cannot be utilised for anti-trust competitive purposes.

The third type of group company is one constituted by contract and it is essentially when one company agrees to subordinate its management to another company. Should such an unusual step be recommended by the board of directors of the company surrending its management decisions, the dominant company must acquire the equity interests of the quota or shareholders. Various legal formalities are required.

Individual Establishment of Limited Responsibility

In 1986, by Decree Law 248/86, there was created for the first time in Portugal the "Individual Establishment of Limited Responsibility" or E.I.R.L. as it is denoted in Portugal. Admittedly, this is a business form unlikely to be used by a significant investor as it was intended for the average merchant who had previously operated in his own name with unlimited responsibility. The object of the law enacted in 1986 was to encourage modest venture capital without the risks of unlimited liability. The basic requirement of this innovating decree law was to require the merchant to have a deed before a notary, declare the amount of capital involved (which cannot be less than 400,000 Esc. and it is obligatory that this capital not be mixed into the private affairs of the E.I.R.L. Should this happen, then the merchant will have lost the benefits of limited liability and find himself liable as if he were a sole proprietor. The business must have a firm name and carry the designation E.I.R.L. There are the usual requirements of publication and registration. The law provides for augments of capital.

In order to stimulate and improve the activities of companies and to encourage mutual efforts towards market efficiency and technological research, laws were enacted in 1973 permitting companies to act together with the designation of

A.C.E., meaning complementary grouping of companies. Such associations could benefit from fiscal incentives. However, the laws in question, Law No. 4/73 and Decree Law 430/73 state that such groupings shall not have as their principal activity the obtaining of profits, although this may exist. The A.C.E. has more interest for companies already operating in Portugal.

Quota Companies

The most widely used business forms in Portugal are the corporation (called "sociedade anonima" abbreviated "S.A." or "S.A.R.L."), the private limited liability company ("sociedade por quotas" or "limitada", abbreviated "Lda.") and the branch which is discussed below, p.64.

The S.A. is a familiar legal structure to the international investor and lawyer and will be discussed in detail in subsequent paragraphs, for as the modern-day corporation has taken on multi-country activities, it has also become the most easily understood.

However, there is no doubt that the most prevalent form of business organisation used is the Lda. and it is precisely this type of legal form which seems to be most difficult for investors to understand, particularly those businessmen familiar with Anglo-Saxon legal traditions. The greatest difficulty seems to lie not in the details (minimum capital, etc.) but rather in understanding the nature of the Lda. itself.

After forming an Lda. the writer has frequently been asked, even by general counsel for the foreign investor, to forward the shares or their equivalent to the headquarters of the home country. This is not possible because they do not exist. How, then, can a foreign investor be sure that he is the owner of a company without receiving physical or tangible documents in his hand which can be endorsed and transferred?

In Portugal, a company, whatever its form, is created by going to the public notary's office and there, with the parties or their legally constituted representatives, signing the articles of the company before the notary who will first read them to all interested parties. After all parties have signed the articles, called in Portugal "the deed", the notary then signs and with this signature the company is born. There may be many subsequent legal formalities, particularly in the area of public announcements in journals and registrations at the Commercial Registry, but the company comes into existence as soon as the deed is signed.

In the case of an S.A. shares may be delivered. In the case of an Lda. nothing is delivered. The deed of constitution of the Lda. will recite the capital of the company, to whom it belongs and in what percentages. A legal copy of this deed, provided by the notary, is used to register at the Commercial Registry both the formation of the company and the ownership of each participation.

For company records a legal or simple photocopy of the deed is sufficient to provide the foreign investor with complete information as to the articles of his company and its ownership. Ownership in an Lda. is not dependent on physical possession of the deed. Losing a copy of the deed has no importance. Delivering or endorsing such a deed to a third party equally has no importance (other than as evidence, perhaps, of a contract of sale). The only way for a foreign investor to transfer his quota (his interest in the Lda.) is to return to the notary and execute a deed of transfer of quota signed by the seller and the buyer.

Given that an Lda. is more simple in legal structure and given that the legal minimum is rather low by international standards (400,000 escudos), it is normally the preferred choice of the foreign investor other than the large multinational making a substantial investment.

The Lda. requires:

(a) a minimum capital of 400,000 escudos with at least 50% paid in immediately, the balance to be paid in within a maximum of five years;

(b) at least two "partners" are necessary, being called "socios" in Portuguese. The two partners may be collective entities and quite often multi-nationals use two or more subsidiaries as partners;

(c) articles of association are drawn up corresponding to what are sometimes described by Anglo-Saxon lawyers as articles of incorporation or by-laws. Although in legal theory the articles of association could refer generically to "internal regulations" to be drawn up in the future, in practice this raises many problems both with the notary, who must approve the articles, and with the Registrar of the Commercial Registry who has power to review the articles before registering them. (Some years ago the writer recalls having articles of association approved by the notary, which made reference to internal rules "to be established". These were signed by the notary and then taken to the Registrar for registration. The Registrar refused registration, claiming the notary had exceeded his authority and that there could be no reference in the articles of association to rules "to be established" since the public would have no means of knowing these rules. Faced with this parallel authority the writer had little choice but to return to the notary and amend the articles.) It is clear therefore that both the notary and the Registrar will wish to see all applicable articles and rules set out in the initial document. Of course, a company for internal purposes may have its own operating regulations, but these will have no legal effect on third parties;

(d) The management of an Lda. also warrants some discussion since once a company is formed one of the key issues is how the company will be managed and in what

> form. The large institutional investor is used to dealing with a board of directors. The law establishing corporations provides for the creation of a board of directors, but the law establishing an Lda. refers only to "... one or more managers ..." and makes no specific reference to a board of directors.

The management of an Lda. and an S.A. is regulated by the Code of Commercial Societies. In relation to an Lda. there is a specific chapter entitled "Management and Fiscalisation". Naturally, after a multi-national has formed a local subsidiary, it will proceed to designate a manager(s). This creates a practical problem which should be resolved in the articles of association. In Portugal, creditors and banks will wish to deal with a legal representative of the subsidiary and this can only be established in two ways: either the articles of association indicate the precise identity of the managers (which is not a good technique) or the articles stipulate a means of providing a power of attorney to a third party who can legally represent the company. The practical difficulty with the first method is that individual managers come and go and if a particular manager(s) is named in the articles, then every time there is a change of management there must be a new deed before a notary to amend the articles. The simpler technique is to state in the articles that the manager shall be chosen by one specific partner (e.g. the partner holding almost all the capital) or by both partners and that this partner(s) shall designate the manager by a simple power of attorney issued to the individual in question. This means that, when managers change, it is only necessary to execute another power of attorney or pass a resolution.

In legal theory it is possible to create in the articles of association a "board of management" and establish how it will function. For example, the articles can provide for the creation of a "board of managers elected by the partners composed of three members". Thereafter, in the resolution book of the Lda. a resolution can be passed indicating the individual members of the board and their powers. A copy of this resolution would then be furnished to the company's bank(s) and to any third parties making inquiries as to who has powers to bind the company.

One of the consequences of Portugal joining the Common Market has been to compel changes in the commercial law in keeping with the general harmonisation of community law. Thus, influenced by the EEC's directives on company law, an Lda. in Portugal may or may not establish an auditing board (actually called a "fiscal council" in the law) to review the company accounts annually. However, if any two of the following criteria are met for two consecutive years, then Article 262 of the Code requires the nomination of a statutory auditor. The three relevant criteria are:

- total balance sheet assets: 140m escudos;
- total sales and other income: 280m escudos;
- average number of employees during the accounting year: 50.

Another recent innovation in Lda. law has been the compulsory deposit with the Commercial Registry of the annual accounts, although this is dispensed with in the case of those companies not fulfilling the requirements of Article 262. However, given the low thresholds of that article, we can anticipate greater economic transparency in relation to Lda. companies similar to that existing with stock corporations.

Stock Corporations

Characteristics

Substantial investments will generally lead the investor or his counsel to choose the S.A., since this is a legal form with common characteristics both in Europe and the Anglo-Saxon commercial world. Consequently, to appreciate the interrelationship of competition law with company law, some elementary knowledge of the Portuguese stock corporation will be necessary. The following are the basic characteristics of an S.A.:

(a) a minimum of five shareholders is necessary;
(b) the minimum capital is 5m escudos with 30% being paid up by incorporation, this being proved by having the required amount deposited at a bank;
(c) as with an Lda., the formation of a stock corporation takes place before a notary, who will request production of all the necessary licences and documents;
(d) the stock corporation is governed by two alternate systems referred to below;
(e) shares may be bearer or registered and ordinary or preferred;
(f) the decisive governing body is the shareholders' general assembly which can elect and dismiss the board of directors;
(g) the stock corporation must have an auditing board or, if the share capital is less than 20m escudos, an auditor;
(h) accounts are published and this includes the balance sheet, profit and loss statement, report of the board of directors, report of the auditors and minutes of the shareholders meeting approving the accounts;
(i) the board of directors is the supreme administrative body and the general shareholders' assembly is the supreme governing body.

Administration

The administration and fiscalisation of a Portuguese stock corporation can be structured by two different methods, chosen by the shareholders, according to Article 278 of the Code of Commercial Societies (CSC):

(a) board of directors and a fiscal council; or
(b) board of directors, general council and a certified public accountant.

Of these two models, the board of directors and a fiscal council is the more traditional. The second—Article 278(b)—is inspired by the German model, already adopted in 1966 in the French law of commercial societies. This model envisages the general council nominating and dismissing directors without having to call a shareholders' meeting. "Directors" as understood in Article 278(b), means working division heads or department supervisors and Article 278(b) is thus ideally suited for large multidimensional multinational companies.

Payment of Initial Share Capital

The initial deferral of share capital mentioned above cannot be delayed for more than five years. However, this delay only becomes legally triggered when the corporation through the board of directors advises the delinquent shareholders to effect payment within a period of not less than 90 days; thereafter, the unpaid shares will revert to the corporation.

Classification of Shares

Under Portuguese law, shares cannot be issued for less than their nominal value. Shares can be either bearer or nominative. However, the shares must be nominative when there is any restriction on their transfer or if they are not fully paid up. Unless the articles of association dictate to the contrary, bearer and nominative shares can be converted from one form to the other.

In theory there are no limits to the types of shares which may be recognised. Article 302 of the CSC states that diverse "... rights inherent to shares issued by the same society" may be recognised. Types of shares specifically mentioned by the CSC are: ordinary shares, preferred shares, shares without a right to vote (not more than 5% of the share capital) and shares subject to call. But this classification is not exhaustive. The use of shares without a right to vote is normally a way of publicly owned companies attracting savings where the anticipated dividend may exceed the prevailing interest rate on private or governmental bonds.

Restrictions on Transfer

As indicated above, only nominative shares can be subject to a restriction on transfer and the only restriction envisaged by Article 328 of the CSC is submission of the transfer to the consent of the company or to specified conditions which are in the company's interests. What is contemplated by this Article is the situation where a family forms a stock corporation and it is not in the interest of family members to have outsiders in the corporation. In a country where substantial tracts of land are held by families and where deaths have created multiple heirs, often the only sensible way to administer a large estate is through a corporate structure with inherited interests represented by shares in the capital. A refusal of consent to a transfer obligates the company itself to purchase the shares in question.

General Assembly of Shareholders

The general assembly of shareholders must convene in the first three months of each year. A "board of the general assembly" is created with a president and secretary to preside over the meeting and to record its activities. Beyond the annual obligation, a general assembly must be convened when requested by shareholders representing 5% of the social capital or at least 1,000,000 escudos. A shareholder need not be present but his right to grant a proxy to a third party is limited under Portuguese law to his or her spouse, ancestor, descendant, member of one of the administrative boards of the company or another shareholder. In order to prevent abuse of proxies, the Portuguese CSC limits representation of more than five shareholders to a specific general assembly and prohibits the company, through any means, from soliciting proxies. Moreover, the members of the fiscal council cannot accept proxies.

Quorum

When thinking of the convocation of a general assembly and the deliberations taken, it is convenient to separate the quorum necessary into two types of quorums: the quorum necessary for there to be a validly constituted assembly and then the quorum necessary for the validly constituted assembly to function. Under the Code of Commercial Societies, the first convocation of a stock corporation which is going to consider matters which may lead to an alteration of the articles, e.g. augment of capital, merger, issue of new classes of shares, can only be validly constituted on the first convocation if at least one-third of the shareholders appear; on the second convocation any number is sufficient.

Once validly constituted, a majority of two-thirds of those present is needed to vote on the topics previously indicated with one exception: if on the second convocation at least half of the shareholders appear, then a simple majority (and not two-thirds) is sufficient for voting. An example will perhaps be helpful. Imagine a stock corporation with 30 shareholders. The quorum rules would function as follows.

For a validly constituted assembly

- First convocation: at least 10 shareholders (one-third);
- Second convocation: any number.

For voting

- First convocation: at least seven (two-thirds of 10);
- Second convocation: two thirds of those present;
- exception: if 15 people appear on the second convocation (half of 30), only eight votes are necessary and not 10 which would be the result if the two-thirds rule were applied.

The only practical reason for such mathmatical complexity appears to be the observed fact that most shareholders appear not on the first convocation but on the second and hence the legislator's desire to lower the voting majority needed (a majority of 15 is eight while two-thirds of 15 is 10).

Voting

Unless the articles of association provide to the contrary, each share has one vote. However, certain variations to this principle are permitted by the articles of association:

- establishing that votes in excess of a certain number shall not be counted if held by only one shareholder. This would appear to prevent institutional investors from dominating a corporation. However, the clause creating this principle obviously cannot be worded to discriminate against one particular class of shareholders.
- equating one vote to a certain number of shares, provided at least 20,000 escudos of capital always has one vote. Thus, the articles could require that in a corporation which has issued shares of a nominal value of 1000 escudos each, 20 shares are required for one vote.

Registration of shares

The CSC permits shares to be subject to any special diplomas compelling registration or deposit in an institution of credit. In actual fact, there was promulgated in 1982 Decree Law 408/82 defining the conditions under which shares had to be registered or deposited. By the terms of this law, all nominative shares of a share corporation or limited partnership with shares must be either registered or deposited at a bank. The law establishes mechanisms for ensuring compliance, one of them being forms to be completed and sent to the tax department when there takes place a subscription or transfer of shares, affecting, of course, nominative shares. For these reasons, nominative shares are more burdensome to negotiate on the stock exchange as there is more paper work to be completed. The question then arises, why would a corporation issue nominative shares if it expects to be quoted on an exchange? One answer is that sometimes the law obliges nominative shares to be issued. This is the case with banks which must have 80% of their capital represented by nominative shares. Investment funds must have all their capital represented by nominative shares. Additionally, any creditor lending money against shares as security would surely want the shares either registered or deposited as in both cases the law allows a security interest to be noted on the accompanying documents. Consequently, while there will exist many inconveniences with nominative shares, their registration or deposit becomes compulsory should they be issued. The registration or deposit of nominative shares also has tax consequences. While dividends on nominative or bearer shares are treated alike, there is a capital gains tax of 10% on the transfer of shares. Nominative shares can not be transferred without complying with various formalities while bearer shares are simply passed from hand to hand.

Outline of Steps to Form a Company

After a decision has been made as to the form of company to be used, the actual constitution of a company in Portugal requires the completion of various bureaucratic steps, in the chronological order indicated below:

(a) obtaining of name which is done by completing a form at the Registo Nacional de Pessoas Colectivas (National Registry of Companies);

(b) filing a form known as a declaration of intent with ICEP which solicits information about the investment, in particular accounting information. The form is basically for statistical purposes as only under very exceptional circumstances could ICEP question the nature of the investment. For example, investments closed to the private sector at present, such as the postal service or railway transport would require special authorisations;

(c) deposit of the capital of the company in the state savings bank (Caixa Geral de Depósitos); it is not always necessary to deposit 100% of the capital but this is dependent on the number of legal variables;

(d) ICEP, after reviewing the information, emits a letter,

with a number on it, acknowledging the registration of the investment, and there are fees to be paid, which are not significant;

(e) this letter, along with the authorisation of the name, and other legal instruments, in particular the proposed articles of association, are taken to the notary where the company is formed;

(f) the articles of the company are registered in the commercial conservatory and published in the official gazette and a local newspaper.

(g) a tax form known as initiation of activity must be filed with the Tax Department to obtain a fiscal number;

(h) the company must also obtain a "commercial number" again by filing a form at the National Registry of Companies;

(i) the minute book and certain accounting books are brought to the tax department and commercial conservatory to be stamped;

(j) a registration must be made with the local social security office.

Incorporation Charges

To form a company in Portugal involves petitioning for the use of a name; a prior declaration to ICEP; notarial fees; stamp tax on capital; publication in journals and registration at the Commercial Registry. Total incorporation charges should not exceed 3% of the capital.

Branch

The choice of a branch by the foreign investor has long been an anomaly under Portuguese law, and more for practical reasons than legal reasons. In theory the law permits the establishment of a branch although formalities are obviously required. These include translation of the company's articles, registration at the Commercial Registry, nomination of a representative or manager, publication requirements, authorisation for the use of a name and of course registration at the local tax department for the area. In themselves, these formalities are little different in terms of time from forming a company. The real obstacle to the formation of a branch in Portugal is the commercial community (including of course the banks) which is used to dealing with a finite local unit with a stated capital and its own Portuguese articles whose meaning is sufficiently commonplace as to be understood locally. Translating into Portuguese the articles of a US corporation might require 30 pages of translation and the language commonly used by American or English draftsmen would not be readily understood in Portugal. It would immediately be thought of as "foreign" or "legally tricky", hardly an auspicious way to start out on a foreign investment.

From the foreign investor's viewpoint, a branch means there is no finite limit in terms of capital beyond which there is no further financial responsibility. In legal theory, all of the assets of the mother company are at risk in relation to the operations of the branch. One would think this comforting prospect might make branches welcome in Portugal but it does not. In the case of a judgment obtained against the defendant branch, it involves execution of the judgment outside Portugal, the outcome of which can be decidedly uncertain.

Nevertheless, a branch does enjoy a specific beneficial tax treatment, namely that the transfer of profits by a branch is not liable to withholding tax, a subject we shall consider in further detail below.

Equity Joint Ventures

It is commonplace for a foreign investor to encounter a local Portuguese partner and each of them, by a capital contribution, form a local Portuguese subsidiary. This frequent commercial event is often loosely referred to as a joint venture but it is different from the contractual joint venture as previously noted. We are, of course, dealing with the equity joint venture.

What are the topics or legitimate concerns which regularly face the foreign investor when he engages in an equity joint venture? They normally fall within the following categories:

(a) ownership and convenient percentage guidelines;
(b) special features to be put in the articles of incorporation;
(c) management of the joint venture;
(d) financial concerns;
(e) local market policies;
(f) side agreements, ranging from know-how to technical assistance;
(g) ownership identity;
(h) settlement of disputes;
(i) law to be applied;
(j) typical contract clauses in areas involving nationals from different countries.

Ownership

A great deal of negotiating time is often spent in attempting to define who shall have majority control or whether it shall be a 50–50 division of capital. We can expect the foreign investor bringing in substantial amounts of capital to want to have the decisive vote. On the other hand, we can certainly appreciate the concerns of the local investor who, besides capital, is contributing his knowledge of local markets and ways of doing business.

In fact, as we shall see later, voting power can be curtailed or augmented. For the moment two simple basic tenets of Portuguese company law should be considered. In a limited company such as a quota company (denominated in Portuguese "sociedade por quotas"), which is by far the most commonly used legal vehicle by foreign investors, 75% of the votes are needed to change the articles of the company. In a share corporation, the familiar "Inc" (S.A.R.L. in Portuguese), there is always present the problem of an assembly functioning with the necessary votes needed (called quorum) and valid deliberations being taken by the majority of those votes present. As a guide, we can think of requiring 75% of the ownership of the capital in a quota company and 51% of the shares of a stock corporation to alter the articles of incorporation. By owning 51% of the capital and appearing at the general assembly, the foreign investor can never be outvoted. Naturally, such percentages of capital result in the application of the rules applied to affiliated companies but our present concern is precisely that: how to enable the foreign investor to control his investment without interference from minority partners.

But why do we care about altering the articles of incorporation? Presumably, upon foundation of the company we have carefully drafted the articles we intend to regulate our internal affairs. It is a consequence of Portuguese law that a merger, an augment of capital or a dissolution and liquidation of a company are considered alterations to the articles of incorporation. These common occurences, therefore, in the life of a commercial company, cannot be taken without the qualified majority demanded by Portuguese law. Consider the foreign investor who wishes to terminate his presence in a company. In a quota company, he cannot do this unless he has 75% of the capital. What about the successful local subsidiary in which a multinational has a 49% ownership of capital? Its expansion plans will be hampered without the consent of the local partners, which consent may be very difficult to obtain for financial reasons or their own lack of vision. Think of the typical situation where a local bank feels the subsidiary is undercapitalised. There will be difficulty in obtaining loans unless the capital is augmented, which legal act requires the afore-mentioned qualified majority of votes. All these are frequent banal ocurrences in the life of a company and cannot be solved by the traditional 51% control of capital in a quota company or 50–50 ownership in a share corporation.

Special Provisions in Articles of Incorporation

Obtaining the necessary majority of capital obviously resolves who "controls" the subsidiary. But very often such total control is not practical nor even financially possible or desirable. Assuming, then, that total control is not possible, the question arises of unanticipated or practical problems and their solutions, which the foreign investor should be aware of.

The most common fear of the non-resident foreign investor is that voting may take place without his knowledge. What good is notice of a general assembly if you never receive it on time? It is therefore extremely useful (and also very comforting) to insert as a special clause in the articles that on certain issues a qualified majority of votes is needed, even if notice has been given. In this case, the qualified majority needed would be those number of votes which must include some of the votes of the foreign investor. In this way, the presence of the foreign investor is needed for any decision taken on certain issues. Of course this is nothing more than modifying the general laws by a provision in the articles. However, so long as this requirement is only selected for special topics (for example augment of capital, mergers, dissolution, election of managers, distribution of profits or otherwise) the other partner is normally prone to accept this condition. Indeed, not to accept it would be to raise a red flag towards a fruitful relationship.

Another very delicate issue, but a very common feature of multinational investments, is when the foreign investor, in addition to furnishing capital, is expecting to sign a contract with the projected joint venture subsidiary. This contract can be as diverse as a distribution contract or a technical assistance agreement for a Portuguese market outlet for computers. What can the foreign investor do to ensure that the equity joint venture subsidiary will honour the contract? Imagine a multinational forms a local subsidiary with a Portuguese investor to install greenhouses throughout Portugal. Besides capital, the foreign investor will also furnish know-how or technical assistance. The importance of the investment for the foreign investor may reside almost exclusively in the fees under the contract and therefore it is imperative that the contract be implemented in good faith. We come now to a special area of Portuguese law: on issues involving themselves, partners are not allowed to vote. We can then imagine a situation (and one I have encountered more than once) where some time after the formation of the local subsidiary the Portuguese partner convokes a general assembly with the following agenda: to consider whether or not there has been a breach of the contract signed by the local subsidiary with multinational USA (a partner in the subsidiary) by the latter entity. Under Portuguese law, multinational USA could not vote on this issue and we can easily imagine the conclusion of the general assembly if we are dealing with a subsidiary composed of only two partners.

After much consideration, the simplest solution I have found is to insert in the articles that any dispute in any contract to which one of the partners is a party shall always be implemented pending a final, non-appealable court decision. While such a provision could be inserted into the contract itself, its breach could lead to endless pedantic legal discussions. Once put in the articles, a vote to the contrary would be null and void which is a much simpler infirmity to attack. In any event, from my own experience, such a provision in the articles invariably dissuades the local Portuguese partner from raising alleged breaches of contract unless there is very good cause, which can happen from time to time.

Management of the Joint Venture

Once formed, the local joint venture must be managed and invariably the excercise of these rights must be carefully drafted so as to reflect the business interests of each party. Although it is common to think that management rights normally bear a logical relationship to the amount of share capital held by each party, there is no legal right why this has to be. In fact, management and ownership are distinct legal concepts and in the structure of the management of a company, the law allows substantial freedom.

We have seen that it is possible to insert in the articles of incorporation provisions requiring a certain amount of votes for any topic considered of vital interest to the investors, e.g. augments of capital. Should negotiations not succeed in obtaining such a provision in the articles of the company, a simple "fall back" position is to require on any particular issue a certain number of directors' votes. In order for this provision to make sense it would be necessary that the articles give to a minority partner the right to elect a certain number of directors.

The latter solution is efficient only in dealing with a stock corporation. With a quota company the problem becomes more complicated. Normally, quota companies are administered by "managers" elected in a general assembly of partners. In order for a minority partner to ensure representation in the management, it would be necessary to create a "board of management", permitted under Portuguese law, or to have the articles state that the company shall be managed by the partners, "with equal representation". Under Portuguese law, there is no impediment to a foreigner occupying a management position. This greatly facilitates the protection of the foreign investor.

Some of the areas in which it is customary to insist upon special voting rules in management are as follows:

(a) augments of capital;
(b) mergers;
(c) dissolution and liquidation;
(d) selection of auditors;
(e) loans to partners;
(f) sale of assets exceeding a certain amount;
(g) alterations to the articles of the company.

If there exist any agreements between the company and one of its partners, e.g. a technical assistance agreement, it would be prudent also to include any alterations, termination or alleged breach of this agreement to require a qualified majority on the board.

Should the partners take the position that to avoid deadlocks on any issue there must be a qualifying vote, or alternatively, there must be a president or chief-executive officer who shall make the final decision in the event of a deadlock, it would be wise to have this office alternate periodically, e.g. every two years.

Financial Concerns

It is usual for the points of view of the foreign investor not to coincide wholly with those of the local investor, particularly if the foreign investor is a multinational with many cross-border activities. The foreign investor may consolidate his multi-country activities and see no immediate advantage in distributing profits lavishly; the shares of the multinational may be quoted on a public exchange and the value of its investment in any one foreign subsidiary finds its way into its share-quotation. Consequently, the foreign investor may have its own particular viewpoint as to what to do with local subsidiary profits, e.g. retain them and build up the value of the subsidiary or distribute as much as possible and strip the subsidiary as it has proved to be a weak investment. The list could be multiplied. It is obvious that while partners from different jurisdictions may have a reason to pool their resources, both material and intellectual, divergences always exist.

The parties involved may therefore wish to ensure that certain standards of financial management are followed. One immediate concern is where such relevant conditions should appear. Should it be in the articles of incorporation? This would render the articles excessively detailed and make difficult changes from one year to another due to the formalities concerned with the amendments of articles. Side agreements between the partners? But this is not so effective in cases of breach, particularly if we are dealing with a stock corporation with many shareholders. One immediate solution would be to put many of the relevant conditions into internal regulations such as by-laws. But by-laws as used in the Anglo-Saxon legal tradition are not used in Portugal although there is in legal theory no prohibition as to their use. The typical Portuguese corporation has its articles of incorporation and nothing more.

Instead, what happens in Portugal is, whether for a quota company or for a stock corporation, every year a general assembly is held and "resolutions" are passed on a variety of matters, including approval of accounts, and thereafter transcribed into a book called "Livro das Actas", which means literally a book of the acts of the partners. Prior to formation of a local joint venture company, it is often extremely useful to get the partners to agree on any restrictions they wish to place on multiple financial items, and simultaneously with the formation of the subsidiary, an "acta" is passed detailing the agreement affecting financial items.

Typical concerns of foreign investors include:

(a) distribution of profit;
(b) working capital requirements;
(c) equity/debt relationship;
(d) expansion goals;

(e) acquisitions;
(f) reserve requirements;
(g) dividend goals;
(h) restriction on management fees or profit-sharing;
(i) accounting procedures to be followed.

Side Agreements

The foreign investor arrives with his capital, his know-how and his side agreements. It is not feasible commercially to form a computer sales subsidiary and not have the technical assistance available to service repairs. Sometimes the repairs are so technical they may have to be referred to another country for service where the foreign investor has another subsidiary. It is common place for the partners to think of the formation of the subsidiary as so many distinct acts: company, partners, agreements, operation. Yet the commercial life of a company is similar to a constellation and to separate one set of legal relations from all others is false because the foreign investor in its pre-country plans envisaged a whole series of legal relations.

The most common problem which arises is when there are side agreements and one of the partners wishes to have the side agreement between the company and the other partner modified or terminated or not even honoured. The most difficult situation arises when the complaining partner insists he can obtain the services locally at a cheaper price and the company should not be penalised.

There is no doubt that many side agreements have different functions and sometimes one of them is to take out profit from the local investment under the guise of "technical fees". From the point of view of the foreign investor, the simplest way to avoid a threatened rupture of contracts is to tie up the side agreement with buy-out requirements. This is a strict standard and admittedly even severe but it accomplishes the object. If the foreign investor would make the investment whether or not there existed the side agreements, then such commercial harshness can be forgotten. But if the investment is seen as a total package with any side agreements forming an integral part of same, then simultaneously with the formation of the subsidiary appropriate buy-out agreements should be drawn up, included in the side agreement and requiring the other party to purchase the shares or quotas if for any reason the side agreement is not renewed.

Ownership Identity

This section is concerned not with restrictions on transfer of ownership but with changes in the identity of the owners, a different sort of problem. Most investments in a foreign country are preceded by commercial experience with a local company and through this experience the foreign investor decides to increase his presence, usually through the formation of a subsidiary. The typical pattern is that a distribution contract is replaced by the formation of a subsidiary with the distributee now becoming a partner with his original supplier.

In these cases, confidence has normaly been created between the parties and the success of the equity joint venture depends on this continuity. The legal theory that companies outlive their founders is a partial truth, for while the company may survive it may be the mere shadow of the dynamic organisation it once was. For this reason, it becomes crucial and of paramount importance to separate out two problems: (a) how to prevent shares being sold to a third party not known to the investor, and (b) to ensure a device to the foreign investor of being able to disengage itself from the local investment. This latter contingency can be triggered by any number of events: death, retirement, proposed transfer of shares, court seizure of local investor's interests for credit purposes, reversal of public image of local investor. In view of the wide variety of reasons which may change the foreign investor's opinion as to whether it wishes to continue in the local investment, our problem becomes to delineate what is the simplest legal device for coping with such changed circumstances. How, in short, can the foreign investor disengage when it wants to? And how can the foreign investor prevent the entry of partners it had not contemplated?

Preventing the entry of third party partners is easier to resolve. It is commonplace for articles of a company to have written into them restrictions on the transfer of shares or quotas. Such restrictions, *per se*, are of dubious value under Portuguese law. Such clauses have some value, but it is more in the nature of dissuasion. This conclusion is a result of Portuguese law which allows the company articles to prohibit transfers but then obliges the company to purchase the shares for sale upon the same terms and conditions as the offer the seller has received. In legal theory this seems fair but it leads to wide abuses and it is an impossible standard to fiscalise. It is not difficult to arrange a simulated offer upon exaggerated terms. The restrictions in the articles can only be effective when coupled with another right granted to the company.

This is to oblige the offeree to sell his interest at a *discount* and then the company may resell the purchased interest to the same party at a profit. The company's right to purchase would have to be subject to confirming the alleged buyer is ready and able to purchase. This will discourage immensely simulated offers. And if the offer was not simulated, what is the justification for the discount? Probably none, unless we believe that the discount rate is equal to the exaggeration rate. In any event, it is a clause which may appear draconian but does eliminate many bogus offers made in the hope of blackmailing the foreign investor to paying above the fair market value.

What has been said above about restrictions on transfer to third parties is also applicable, although in modified form, to the right of first refusal. Instead of the articles prohibiting transfers without the consent of the company, the articles can grant to the company the right of first refusal. But this is a distinction of no great practical importance in Portugal since under Portuguese law the power of the company to refuse to give its consent obliges it to purchase the shares. It is in effect a right of first refusal. Consequently, although in legal theory there is a difference between granting consent and having the right of first refusal, in practical terms it is a distinction of minor interest.

The problem of how the foreign investor can disengage itself from its investment raises the question of exoneration rights granted by the articles of a company. Under Portuguese law, the right to compel the company to purchase your shares or quotas is called exoneration rights and it is the equivalent of a "put" in financial terms. However exoneration rights are only expressly recognised for quota companies. For stock corporations, such a right would have to be the subject of a side agreement with the other shareholders. Obviously, this is only workable in a small, closed corporation. Exoneration rights rarely figure in quota company articles and yet they provide and effective means for disengagement by the foreign investor. Typical statutory reasons which would allow the foreign investor to compel the company to buy its quota could be as varied as adverse tax legislation, nationalisation, capital market restrictions, change of key personnel, to name but a few. Exoneration rights are a powerful tool for the foreign investor and their use should be more frequent.

Litigation

One common problem is how to resolve disputes between the partners. If we are dealing with a foreign investor, this is particularly acute as the foreign investor may not have any familiarity with the legal system of the host country. The most usual ways are:

(a) resolution by officers of each investor;

(b) arbitration;
(c) court proceedings;

If we are dealing with multinationals or large companies with a great deal of commercial experience, a simple way of handling disputes is to have an agreement reached, whether put in the "acta" or by an independent agreement, that all disputes shall first be presented to the board of directors or an officer of each party. Without any actual language being suggested as a guideline, suffice to say that the intent is that all disputes shall first be put to the superior hierarchies of each partner for an attempted resolution. While this may sound too informal, in practice it is very effective. Disagreements often arise at a local subsidiary level and by the time the superior levels of the partners hear of the dispute it is already in court.

Both arbitration and the law courts have their virtues and disadvantages. Joint ventures of a technical nature are probably best served by arbitration while for marketing joint ventures the law courts may be better, but this is seeing the problem from the viewpoint of the foreign investor. In the law courts, there is less likelihood of the principles of equity or good conscience being invoked and while these are sensible principles of conduct their application in a commercial dispute becomes a never-ending moral search for who has more right on his or her side. Consequently, in the traditional commercial joint venture, the law courts narrow the disputes to clear legal issues. For those who prefer arbitration, there is the Center of Commercial Arbitration, functioning and supported by the Commercial Association of Lisbon, with its offices at Rua das Portas de Santo Antõ, 89P, 1194 Lisboa Codex.

Lex Loci

Most agreements that are sent to me by foreign investors and meant to serve as operating agreements with the local investor state that all disputes shall be resolved by the law of the foreign investor. I cannot think of a more troublesome clause passing for wisdom. Assuming that the local partner accepts such a clause, how will the law of England be proved to a Portuguese judge? Only by expert testimony and this is a complicated procedure. Even if it can be done, you are asking a judge or arbitrator to listen to a case day after day and have no general legal reference for the material he is studying. The law cannot be viewed in so narrow a prism and it is the wiser investor who takes the trouble to acquaint himself with the generalities of Portuguese law and accepts the application of its laws. In this way, the local Portuguese investor–partner is well aware of the implications of his acts and the general commercial law of Portugal is founded on principles of law as sensible as those of other developed legal communities.

In fact, Article 3 of the Code of Commercial Societies obliges companies with their article headquarters in Portugal to be subject to Portuguese law and while various devices may be encountered to avoid this sensible rule, it is best to accept its application.

Typical Equity Venture Clauses

Invariably, an equity joint venture is preceded by a detailed joint venture agreement. Admist all the details it is worth remembering certain precautionary clauses which should be present.

The most important clause which should be carefully drafted is the reason for the joint venture. Why have the parties decided to form a company? Such a clause is often extremely valuable in the event of litigation for reasons not foreseen at the initial stages of the joint venture and the statement of principles upon which the joint venture was initially formed serves as a guideline for judges and others who have to interpret and resolve problems not foreseen or contemplated.

A further clause which goes a long way to heading off disputes is one which obliges the parties to cooperate and deal in good faith. While these moral strictures may seem out of place in a commercial agreement, the Civil Code of Portugal imposes the obligtion of good faith on all contractual parties and seeing this obligation set forth in writing is morally persuasive. It avoids litigation. It is one of those vague philosophical statements from which everyone draws comfort and makes the other side less sure.

It is also wise to have an English and Portuguese version of the contract and both versions are binding on the parties. As to the prevailing version, if there is litigation in Portugal, it will be the document used. The reason for having two versions approved, English (or other language of the foreign investor) and Portugese, is to avoid one party claiming not to understand the natural reading of the clause in question. It avoids the defence of "I thought this clause meant something else" or worse, "In English, these words have an entirely different meaning". With each party having a good translation into his own language of the joint venture agreement, language disputes are effectively put aside.

Finally, the most helpful clause of all is a statement that the principles of the joint venture agreement supersede the formation of the company and its general principles shall be used as reference in the event of any litigation. The utility of this clause has been mentioned above. But it is important that it should survive and not be considered "buried" with the creation of the subsidiary. For this reason, a "survival" clause is most helpful.

In concluding this part on equity joint ventures the following checklist covers the items which should be the concern to the foreign investor as he starts to plan his investment:

(a) the reason for the investment which should be the subject of a detailed joint venture agreement;

(b) the legal form the company will take. Once this is decided then there must be considered the following items;
(c) amount of capital;
(d) any special voting rights;
(e) management rights if investor has a minority interest;
(f) any special quorum requirements for the general assembly to ensure protection for the foreign investor;
(g) financial aspects such as reserves, dividends, budgets, which may not be a natural consequence of the law;
(h) marketing plans as to future courses of action which should also be established in the joint venture agreement or in a resolution upon formation of the equity joint venture;
(i) escape clause for the foreign investor should he wish to disengage himself from the investment, e.g. side agreements with the other partners or a clause in the joint venture agreement indicating the conditions under which the foreign investor can oblige either the company or the other investors to purchase his investment;
(j) auditing requirements such as the firm shall use an internationally known firm of auditors;
(k) governing law if there are disputes and how they shall be resolved.

Minority Interests

Any foreign investment naturally invites the search for what protection, if any, Portuguese law confers upon minority interests. The foreign investor does not always purchase or have a controlling interest. The special treatment that minority interests receive under the CSC may be summarised as follows:

(a) transparency rules under inter–company relationships, have been discussed above, p.48. CSC 484; however, another section of the CSC requires an owner of 10, 33.3 or 50% of the bearer shares of a company to advise the company of this ownership (CSC 448);

(b) there is the possibility of a 10% minority owner compelling purchase of his shares (see above, p.49. CSC 490);

(c) there is a right to information (see below, p.80.);

(d) additionally, although not strictly a minority right, there exists the right to profit (see below, p.83);

(e) there are also other rights, again not minority rights as such but used by minority groups to protect their interests, i.e. voting syndicates whereby shareholders contract with each other to vote on a certain issue uniformly. Voting syndicates are permitted by CSC 17 and are discussed below, p.84;

However, the much-used cumulative right given in many countries to shareholders is flatly prohibited by CSC 384.

The new Code of Commercial Companies published in 1986 established for Ldas and S.A.s what is entitled the "right to information". In quota companies, there are no minimum percentages established for requesting information. Article 214 obliges the manager of an Lda. to give to "... any partner ... " truthful and complete explanatory information about the management of the company. This obviously includes "... information about acts already carried out ...". These rights are further amplified so that the inquiring partner can have his auditor examine the accounts. The only limitation on these rights, imposed by Article 215, is that refusal of the right of information will be valid if the information requested is to be used for purposes "... alien to the company ..." and prejudicial to it. Also if disclosure involves violating an obligation of confidentiality imposed by law.

The right to information granted to shareholders in corporations is not so straightforward, due no doubt to the legislators' realisation that large public corporations are often the target of frivolous requests. In some respects the right to information in corporations is more precise in legal terms but it is subject to quantitative limitations.

Pursuant to Article 291, "... shareholders whose shares attain 10% of the capital are able to solicit, in writing, ... information about social matters". The word "social" in this context means "company" since in legal theory a company is regarded as a social pact between people regulated by the articles of association. There is also an equivalent right to refuse to provide information, as in the case of Ldas.

The right to information in stock corporations is more specifically defined than in Ldas. Thus, apart from normal accounting information *any* shareholder (there is no minimum requirement as to voting power or shares) can under certain circumstances ask to know the salaries paid to employees and/or members of the board of directors. Any shareholder can of course ask to see all accounting information (the law refers to the last three accounting years). The law also grants the right to consult the share registration book and the resolution book, which may be helpful in cases where a takeover is anticipated.

Judicial Inquiry

The law provides to the owners of capital in a Portuguese company, both stock corporations and quota companies, a certain power of fiscalisation. There are basically two techniques: (1) a judicial inquiry and (2) nomination of a member to the fiscal board.

As indicated previously, the owners (meaning either shareholders or quota owners) have a right to information from the company in which they own capital.

The exact powers of the court are defined in the section on stock corporations (Article 292 *et seq.*) but by reference they also apply to quota companies. There are two situations in which the court can intervene. The first is where the owner has requested information and it has not been provided. Any owner of capital (no minimum amount of capital is required) can, with reference to the last three accounting periods, request from the company management reports, accounting material, resolutions of the general assembly, amounts paid to the members of the administration, salaries paid to the highest paid employees and (without time limit) the register of shares or quotas. If not forthcoming, the aggrieved owner may petition the court for a judicial inquiry.

However Article 291 of the Code of Commercial Companies states that owners may also request information about "social matters". Remembering that the word "social" in Portuguese refers to "company", the code has clearly conferred upon the owners of capital a substantial right, since any matter relevant to the life of the company can form the subject of a request. Recognising the extent of this right, the Code has subjected the use of this power to a minimum capital requirement of 10%. Once this threshold is met, and if the information requested is refused, the court may order an inquiry to obtain the information.

The other broad right given to owners is to nominate a member of the fiscal board, although this right is also subject to a 10% threshold capital requirement. However, once met, minority interests who have their choice of a fiscal board member outvoted may request the court to appoint a further fiscal board member nominated by the minority interests.

The powers of the court when intervening in response to a judicial inquiry are formidable. By virtue of Article 292 of the CSC the powers of the judge range from ordering the information to be provided to nominating a director or administrator and dismissing the persons responsible for the illegal refusal.

Right to Receive Profits

It will perhaps seem strange that the right to receive profits should be included under the subject of protection of minority interests and yet, under Portuguese law, this right is enshrined in Article 21 of the CSC which has been used with success in defending the interests of minority groups. Specifically, Article 21 states that every partner (and no particular type of company is specified so that all business forms will be included) has the right "to participate in the profits". Although the amount of profits to be distributed may be varied by the articles and even by the law (Article 294 of the CSC only requires half of the profits in a stock corporation), there is a clear right to receive *something*.

In a recent case in Portugal, a company, instead of declaring dividends to distribute its profits, called for an increase of capital. The purpose of this, as alleged by the minority interests, was to divert funds for use in another company in which the company in question had a substantial investment. In simple language, owners of capital were seeing their profits diverted to help a company in distress, from which they could only hope to obtain an indirect benefit, since between the owners and the distressed company stood their own company. The court, upon the request of various minority interests, prohibited the increase of capital. Although there were also some other irregularities at issue, one of the main arguments advanced by counsel for the minority interests was precisely this right of an owner to receive his fair share of the profits.

The problems indicated above could have been avoided by the use of Article 11 of CSC which allows the articles of a company to subject participation in other companies to a vote in the general assembly and not be dependent only on the investment decisions of management.

Voting Syndicates

Voting syndicates are now permitted by CSC 17. This is an innovation as prior to the publication of the CSC there was much divided legal opinion whether such syndicates were valid. While the CSC has now explicitly made such arrangements valid, they are not entirely free from many doubts. Specifically, the CSC admits the existence of such agreements but states that such syndicates cannot be used to annul acts of the company. The syndicates only operate between those who have signed the agreement, and presumably any breach of such agreements gives rise only to a cause of action for damages. Compelling votes in accordance with the syndicate appears not to be possible. The voting syndicates are limited to the exercise of the right to vote but cannot affect "... the conduct of the interested parties or of other persons in the exercise of functions of administration or fiscalisation". The article is intended to permit a legal device which can be used to defend minority interests, e.g. multiple owners of small interests agree to pool their votes in an attempt to elect a director.

Accounting Information

One of the innovations of the new company law in Portugal was to require not only stock corporations but quota companies to deposit at the Commercial Conservatory substantial accounting information. Additionally, Article 65 of the Company Law permits the articles of the company to require any further accounting information to be published or made available as deemed necessary by the drafters of the articles of the company. What further information is advisable to warrant being given article articulation?

In small quota companies (small in terms of partners and not capital) and closely held corporations, the following suggestions may help maintain transparency among the partners, a vital ingredient in good working relationships:

- require partners or shareholders to advise what other participations they have in other companies which could possibly have a commercial influence on the company in question;
- require the accounts to indicate for anyone in a management position all other fees or commissions earned through other activities from any source which might be a potential client of the company in question. If it were a competitor, it would be prohibited by the norms of the Portuguese law.

The Securities and Exchange Act 1991

On 10th April 1991 there was signed into law a comprehensive and extensive code with 686 articles, not including transitory articles, as well as a pedagogic introduction presenting the reasons for the code and its principal objectives. It is intended to be a working legal document for future decades. It is encyclopaedic in format and objectives. It is a fundamental source for anyone interested in the securities market in Portugal and how it functions. In Portuguese, the code is entitled "Codigo do Mercado de Valores Mobiliarios". Translated literally, it means "Code of the Market for Moveables with Value", meaning by moveables that which is not real estate or a fixture, a distinction forming part of Portuguese law as it does also in Anglo-Saxon law. However, the literal translation is cumbersome and hardly indicates what is being regulated, i.e. securities and the function of the exchange market. In English, such a code would be entitled "Securities and Exchange Act" and hence the use of an expression in English which conveys more accurately the purpose of the code, which is abbreviated hereafter as the S&E Act.

We should be grateful for the elucidative effort made by the authors of the S&E Act who admittedly culled much material from relevant American, English and common Market law, at least to the extent of being familiar with it and consciously utilising, or otherwise, the material studied. The introduction lists the following main objectives of the new S&E Act:

(a) to withdraw government intervention and liberalise the securities market;
(b) regulation of the "over the counter" market;
(c) the creation of a securities and exchange commission entitled "CMVM";
(d) the defence of the public interest regarding offers of subscription and sale;
(e) information requiring "full disclosure";
(f) a new regime applicable to takeovers;
(g) prohibition on insider trading;
(h) modernisation of the functioning of the exchanges.

The functioning of the commission, the exchanges, and the "over the counter" market are topics which require detailed explanation of interest only to specialised investors in the financial services, and they are not covered here. Instead, the analysis is concentrated on topics of general interest to the foreign investor.

Ambit

The S&E Act is applicable to all securities emitted, negotiated or commercialised in the national territory. By securities is meant: shares, bonds, titles of participation and any other values, whatever their form, even if only book-keeping entries, whether emitted by private or public entities, susceptible of being negotiated in an organized market.

Information

The S&E Act imposes a substantial burden upon those engaged in financial services. Specifically, information furnished to the public under any form by entities responsible for public offers of subscription or transaction must be in conformity with "... rigorous principles of licitude, truth, objectivity, opportunity and clarity".

Furthermore, the S&E Act establishes a standard of honety and fair play which is probably utopian and intended to defend the investor from any deviousness. To wit, the entities involved shall not "induce" the public in error by the insufficiency, inexactness or falsity of information; by the manner or way in which presentations of information are given; by the omission of facts; or by any circumstances whose knowledge should be reasonably known. The public must be informed of the reality of the "... facts, situations, activities, results, business, perspectives, values, rates of return or of the valuation of capital invested or any other materials that are object of the information".

This laudable standard is also applicable to publicity concerned with emissions and transactions of securities. Additionally, when accounting material appears in a prospectus, the accuracy of these accounts must be certified by chartered accountants registered for this purpose with the CMVM. These same auditors are subject to civil responsibility to the investor for any negligence in their analysis of the accounts.

Subscriptions in the Primary Market

The primary market is where public subscriptions take place for the first time. Subscriptions in the primary market, i.e. offers of sale of shares for subscribing to the initial shares of a stock corporation, are not dependent on any administrative authorisation. However, subscriptions in non-escudo currencies, or by non-residents, or in foreign exchanges by Protuguese companies, may be subject to authorisation, such power being expressly conceded to the Ministry of Finance.

Shares whose rate of return is conditional on reference to an index can also be made subject to special authorisation.

Public Subscription

The S&E Act distinguishes between a public and private subscription and this review is concerned with public subscription. It is worth examining carefully the concept of public subscription since a great deal of investment activity takes place in this area.

A public subscription exists when the shares are offered:

(a) to an inderterminate number of persons; or
(b) to a determined number of persons not previously identified; or
(c) through any means of commercialisation.

Public commercialisation shall be deemed to exist when the subscription is made:

(a) through financial intermediaries to the public;
(b) through publicity in brochures, circulars, etc. to the public;
(c) direct marketing to the public.

There is also considered to exist a public subscription of shares of a company quoted on the exchange even if the subscription is limited to the actual shareholders.

Important exceptions to the above rules are shares created by augments of capital through incorporation of reserves; shares resulting from mergers; or conversion of credits into shares.

Registration of Public Subscription

The S&E Act adopts the legal methodology of a prior registration for all emissions, whether for constitution of a company or *a posterior*, public subscription. This is done by a petition to the CMVM which must be signed by the representatives of the company, or promotors, and by the financial institutions responsible for placing the shares with the public.

The S&E Act is quite detailed as to the contents of the petition and generally requires (indicating only some of the items):

- an explication for the reason for the emission;
- relevant resolutions authorising the emission;
- a copy of the articles of company;
- a copy of the commercial registration of the company;
- a copy of the opinion of the fiscal board;
- a copy of the contract signed with the financial institution handling the placement;
- specimen of the shares;
- a copy of the proposed prospectus;
- a copy of the proposed public announcement;
- a statement by the representatives of the company that from the close of the accounts to the date of petition there has been no material alteration of facts;
- a report by the auditors as to the financial and economic situation of the issuer.

Public Announcement

The proposed public announcement must also contain certain obligatory material, the more important being:

- the price of the subscription and the conditions of payment;
- the terms and conditions of the offer;
- the criteria to be used if there is over-subscription;
- any special conditions to accompany the offer of subscription.

Prospectus

The standard adopted by the S&E Act concerning the contents of the prospectus is one determined to require full and fair disclosure. In the words of the Code, the prospectus must contain all the information:

"1. ... reasonably necessary for the investors be able to for-

> mulate a sound opinion about the activities, the patrimony, the financial situation, the results, the perspectives and all further relevant information ... so the investor can evaluate the investment and the risk involved ...
> 2. The information in the prospectus must be true, complete, objective, technically precise, systematically adequate, exposed in a clear and express form in accessible language ..."

The prospectus and announcement of the offer must be published in a journal of major circulation as well as in one of the bulletins of quotations of the Lisbon or Porto Exchange.

For the sufficiency, veracity, objectivity and timeliness of the information in the prospectus, the Code makes responsible the issuer, the board of directors, the fiscal council, the auditor(s) and the financial institutions.

Rejection or Withdrawal of Subscription

The CMVM can obviously refuse to register the proposed emission if there is a failure to furnish the many documents required. Moreover, the CMVM can refuse the registration if it feels the investor is not adequately protected due to lack of correct information or lack of objectivity or if the information furnished is incomplete. This does not mean that the CMVM, when approving the registration, is certifying that the subscription is a good investment. What it is certifying is that the elements of full disclosure have been made and the persons furnishing the financial and accounting information have a high duty of responsibility to the general public for which they will be held accountable.

Takeovers

Introduction

With the publication of the S&E Act 1991, the entire theory of public takeovers (denominated "OPA" in Portuguese) was changed. Whereas under the previous law an OPA was launched by communicating the same to the targeted board of directors, the new law establishes a different, extremely detailed methodology. In general, an OPA is launched by a prior registration with the CMVM and simultaneously advising the targeted company of the proposed conditions of the takeover. There is no requirement for governmental approval of the OPA other than the registration with the CMVM. Once the targeted board of directors has received notice of the proposed, although as yet unregistered, OPA, it is prohibited from engaging in a series of acts which might be loosely classified as defence measures.

The S&E Act is pre-emptory in its limitations on the power of the targeted board of directors. CSC Article 575 prohibits the board of directors, after they have received notice of the preliminary proposed announcement, from practising any acts other than the usual administration and prohibits the board from initiating any actions or creating conditions which might affect the success of the launched bid. Specifically the following are forbidden:

(a) to emit shares or bonds convertible into shares;
(b) to emit bonds which grant the right to subscribe to shares;
(c) to sell or otherwise alienate the exploration of a sector or significant parcel of the target company's business;
(d) to sell or acquire participations in other companies;
(e) to realise mergers or decapitalisations or sign agreements to this effect.

The philosophy behind this article appears to be the legislator's conviction that public bids are healthy and of value to the consumer (read shareholder). The law is too recent for any comments to be made on the success of this article abridging defences to hostile takeovers.

Object of OPA

Offers destined to purchase shares, or bonds convertible into shares or bonds which confer the right to subscribe to shares, if public, are subject to the rules established in the S&E Act. There are two important exceptions. If the acquisition foreseen is of an insignificant quantity, the CMVM can dispense with the public offer. More importantly, if the offer is for less than 20% of the outstanding shares, there is no need for a regulated public offer. An amount less than 20% can be purchased on the exchange and not be subject to an OPA.

Definitions

An offer is considered public when it meets the conditions described above, p.88. in connection with public subscriptions. For the purpose of prohibiting trading in the shares in question once a registration is made with the CMVM, the concept of bidder is expanded to include not only the offeror, but companies belonging to the same group (see above, p.46 *et seq.*), members of the board of directors, the financial intermediary or any third party having a syndicate of voting with the offeror.

Mandatory OPA

An OPA must be launched whenever there is a purchase or accumulation of shares falling within CSC 313. This is laid down in the S&E Act, Article 527. Under CSC 313 an OPA must occure when:

- the shares concern a public company;
- the shareholders have no right of preference; and
- the purchaser already has shares which assure domination of the targeted company, or with the anticipated

purchase; or the proposed purchase secures at least 20% of the voting power of the targeted company.

In any of the above situations, if the shares already purchased or about to be purchased grant more than 50% of the voting power, then an OPA must be launched for all of the shares, S&E Act, Article 528. Consequently, while an OPA may be made for a limited quantity justifying such an operation (S&E Act, Article 523), it must be launched for all of the shares if Article 528 is applicable.

There are important exceptions to these general principles when dealing with mergers, procedures in bankruptcy and amortisation of shares. In the case of a mandatory OPA, the question naturally arises: how shall the offer price be determined? The S&E Act establishes a minimum reference which is the price the mandatory purchaser paid during the preceding 12 months for the same shares. In case of any doubts, the CMVM will assign an independent expert to determine the fair value.

Preliminary Announcement

Once the bidder has made his decision to launch a public offer, it must send to the targeted board of directors and the CMVM a copy of the proposed public announcement. The contents of the proposed announcement are similiar to those of the public subscription (see above, p.89). The targeted board of directors has eight days to send their comments concerning the proposed offer to the CMVM. Obviously, the CMVM can order changes to the proposed announcement as well as prohibit the announcement if founded upon violations of any of the requirements of the S&E Act. But the approval of the announcement does not mean the registration is complete.

Registration of OPA

Jointly with the sending of the proposed announcement, the proposed bidder must deliver multiple documents to the

CMVM which, among other things, demonstrate corporate authority for the proposed launch. Other documents that must be delivered are proof that the purchase price has been deposited with a financial institution, a copy of the proposed prospectus, proof that the proposed announcement has been set to the targeted company and a copy of the proposed contract with the financial intermediary. A complete list is set forth in Article 539 of the S&E Act.

Report of Targeted Company

The reason for obliging the bidder to inform the board of directors of the targeted company is so that the reaction of the board can be communicated to its shareholders who will then be able to take a rational decision. On the one hand, the S&E Act prohibits the board of the targeted company from taking any unusual management steps and on the other hand obliges it to furnish a great deal of information to the shareholders whose shares are being sought.

Specifically, Article 553 of the S&E Act requires the board of the targeted company to, among other things, to advise the shareholders:

- about the implications of the offer;
- its objectives and the value of the proposed purchase;
- about comments on all the documents presented by the bidder;
- if any agreement exists between the board and the bidder.

CMVM Reaction

The CMVM can refuse the petition for registration; or require further clarification; or allow the registration advising the parties involved. It can also suspend all operations in the exchange concerning the shares in question.

Counter Offer

Once an offer has been registered and then launched, the CMVM will authorise a period of 30–40 days during which the offer is held open. Until one day prior to the last day, a counter-offer can be made which must be for at least a difference of 5% of the first offer. This counter-offer is also subject to registration at the CMVM although with reduced time periods involved. Within eight days of the launching of the counter-proposal, the original offeror must take a stance, either increasing his offer or presenting any other proposals he wishes to make.

Insider Trading

Once a bid has been launched, all insider trading is forbidden. This prohibition extends to:

- the bidder or those acting in concert with the same;
- the board of directors of the targeted company.

Public Offer of Sale

Of the three types of offers to the public envisaged by the S&E Act, i.e. public subscription, hostile takeover (OPA) and public sale, it is the last which has had the most activity in Portugal in recent years. In Portuguese it is denominated "oferta publica de venda" (OPV, meaning a public offer of sale). An OPV is considered public when the conditions described above on p.88 referring to public subscriptions are established. The Ministry of Finance has been granted the power to establish exceptions to the formalism of an OPV when the amounts are minimal, or the offer is destined for a restricted number of persons, or persons by training extremely qualified to evaluate the offer or in fact under any circumstances where an OPV is not deemed justified. However, these important exceptions have not yet been subject to any special legislative attention, and consequently the investor who believes there is no need for an OPV should consult the CMVM. As is the case with public subscriptions and OPAs, there is no requirement of any administrative authorisation. For OPVs also, the only requirement is registration with the CMVM. The OPV must be launched through a financial intermediary which must be responsible for the absorption of the public sale. The shares to be offered must be deposited prior to the public announcement with the responsible financial institution.

Registration

The realisation of an OPV requires it to be registered with the CMVM and this is done by a petition to the CMVM signed by the seller and the financial institution. The petition must be accompanied by much technical and legal information, including the reason for the operation and its objectives. The offer cannot be launched without a copy of the proposed announcement and the prospectus which will accompany the sale also being delivered to the CMVM all of which must be approved by the CMVM. As with the other situations of public sales or acquisitions, the prospectus must contain an auditor's review for which the auditor will assume civil responsibility for the accuracy of the facts contained therein.

Execution of Sale

Once approved by the CMVM, the OPV can take place within 10–30 days. No orders of purchase can be taken within the first five days. a revision of the price can be authorised by the CMVM provided there is a reduction of at least 5%.

Civil Responsibility

The S&E Act exhorts the interested parties to produce a prospectus which is sufficient in facts, true, objective, containing current information and he makes the following persons responsible for failing to adhere to this standard: seller, members of board of directors, members of the fiscal council, persons mentioned in the prospectus as having contributed to the information therein, the auditor and the financial institution.

Labour Law

For the comparative labour lawyer, Portuguese labour law is a hybrid; on the one hand, there are limitations on the employer's right to dismiss; on the other hand, there is no obligatory membership of a union (or syndicate, as it is called in Portugal) and consequently the issue of a union or non-union shop is of no relevance under Portuguese law. Whatever labour contract a syndicate may successfully negotiate will benefit all workers in the same industry. Nor is there any compulsory deduction of dues, this being a voluntary act by the syndicate member. For these reasons Portugal cannot be characterised as a "strongly unionised" country. And yet the syndicates have played a dynamic role in defending the workers and attempting to bring their standards of working conditions up to European standards. A characterisation of the Portuguese labour climate, based on the writer's own experience (ranging from the locking-in of foreign managers shortly after the revolution of 1974 to monitoring of numerous collective dismissals since that time) would portray an educated labour force, reluctant to bring issues to the brink and yet quite cognisant of their rights. With these few general remarks, it will be more instructive, perhaps, to turn to the specific provisions of the law.

Labour Code

The great body of labour law is codified in what is literally translated as the "work contract" and is found in Decree Law 49,408 of 24th November 1969. Students of Portuguese history will immediately wonder how a law made prior to the Portuguese revolution of 1974 can still continue to be in force. In fact, shortly after the revolution, countless decrees were passed which were designed to protect the workers and to prevent mass dismissals. However these were all piecemeal amendments to the general law and Decree Law 49,408 representing the general theory, has never been repealed in its entirety.

The normal interest of the investor, when contemplating setting up in a foreign country, is the extent of his ability to hire and fire; can he expect governmental interference; are there indemnities to be paid upon dismissal; once appointed is the employee an employee for life; in short is the multi-national free to run its business as it wishes?

As one would expect in an EEC Member State such as Portugal the areas of minimum age (18), trial period (15 days normally), working hours (8 hours per day, with a 44 hour working week as now stipulated by Decree Law 2/91 of 17th January, although executives can opt for an unstructured working day without overtime rights), minimum salary (changes every year; as from 1st January 1993 the national minimum salary was 44,500 escudos except for domestic help which was 38,500 escudos), sanitary conditions, labour representation, etc. have all been legislated upon and present no special problems other than a knowledge of the details. However, there are some areas of Portuguese labour law worth commenting on specifically, taking into consideration the questions normally raised by the foreign investor.

Temporary Labour Contracts

The issue of whether an appointment immediately becomes permanent is important as regards indemnities. Under Portuguese law, if a person is protected against dismissal, dismissing him becomes illegal and subject to the payment of indemnities. Consequently, it is important for the foreign investor to know that Decree Law 64-A/89 of 27th February 1989 provides that, in the case of a company starting up operations in Portugal, a temporary labour contract can be validly signed provided the formalities of such a contract are followed. This basically means a written contract identifying the parties, the work to be done, the term, the location, and the professional category of the worker. Provided these legal formalities are complied with, and they are set out in detail in article 42, the execution of a temporary contract is the ideal vehicle for the investor coming to Portugal. In cases of replacement of a worker who is temporarily absent, or for occasional tariffs or special jobs, the temporary contract cannot exceed six months. In all other cases, the employer is free to offer employment for a specific term and to renew the contract provided the total maximum term of the contract does not exceed three years. One important exception is that in the case of the launching of a new activity or the starting-up of a new company, the term of the temporary labour contract is limited to two years, including any renewals. Under these circumstances, there is freedom to employ and to terminate the contract of employment without payment of indemnities. Obviously, due notice has to be given of the termination of the contract in due time; otherwise it will become a contract without term and cannot then be terminated without payment of indemnities.

Terminating Labour Contracts

Once an employee becomes effective, having survived any trial period, Portuguese labour law forbids his dismissal unless there is "just cause". Should the employer believe there to be just cause for dismissal, the labour law provides mechanisms for notifying the employee, so that he may respond, as well as notifying the Worker's Commission. The law also affords the opportunity to the employee to request (by injunctive relief) the suspension of his dismissal and the judge can order such injunctive relief it it appears that the worker has merit to his claim. In Portugal, there are special courts dealing with labour claims and there is a Ministry of Labour and it is not difficult for a worker to obtain legal assistance, either through a syndicate or through the Ministry of Labour who will assign a representative to file the claim in the labour court on behalf of the worker. Given that legal assistance is readily available to a worker, it becomes relevant for the employer to know when dismissal is possible, i.e. when "just cause" will be considered to exist. Article 9 of Decree Law 107/88 of 17th September 1988 indicates that "just cause" will be constituted by:

- disobedience to the orders of the employer;
- violation of the rights and guarantees of the other workers;
- repeated, provoked conflicts with others;
- sustained lack of interest in the work;
- serious injury to the interests of the employer;
- unjustified absence, either for five consecutive days or for ten non-consecutive days in any one year;
- negligence in the observance of hygiene or security at work;
- physical violence against workers or members of the administration;
- abnormal reduction in productivity;
- crimes against the management, including locking them in (a memory left over from the days when workers locked in the management after the 1974 revolution), failure to heed judicial decisions affecting the company and false declarations relative to absence (aimed at curbing the procurement of false medical statements).

In cases where an employee is misbehaving, it should not be difficult to establish the appropriate category of "just cause".

Large-scale Dismissals

Additionally for structural, technological or "business climate" reasons, a company can petition the Ministry of Labour for permission to effect large-scale dismissals, described in Portugal as "collective dismissals". The procedures involved are formal. The Ministry of Labour has wide powers to grant the dismissals, with payment of indemnities, or to allow the petition partially, or to make suggestions as to how to resolve the petitioner's problems without granting the dismissals. It is not a procedure a company would normally undertake except as a last resort in the face of clear and demonstrable economic distress.

Indemnities

It is a peculiarity of Portuguese law that once an illegal dismissal has been established, this does not mean that the payment of indemnities resolves the problem. The writer has had many clients more than willing to pay indemnities to be rid of an employee for one reason or another. And yet the experienced investor will understand that very often employees do not want to be paid off and told to leave. For a variety of reasons, and many of them very understandable, they prefer to retain their employment, even in a hostile atmosphere. For example one multi-national felt its manager was out of touch with the new democratic spirit prevailing in Portugal. Having been employed by the company for approximately 20 years, it was not plausible to find "just cause" (he being the first to arrive and the last to leave). The company tried everything from requiring humiliating work (writing senseless reports) to assigning him to a room never frequented by anyone. No offer of indemnities by the company interested the employee. Nor was the employee obliged to accept any indemnities. In the end it was suggested to the company that the employee be promoted to the board of management where he would have little contact with the workers and his experience could be utilised.

Article 13 of Decree Law 107/88 sanctions this idea by stating that in the case of an illegal dismissal the employee must be reintegrated unless the worker exercises his option to accept indemnities, which amount to one months' pay for each year (or fraction thereof) of service, never being less than three months' pay.

Many companies unaccustomed to doing business in Portugal find this a difficult concept, perhaps because in other countries the employer can oblige the worker to leave if indemnities are paid. This is not the law in Portugal although it must be admitted that very often employees are dismissed without valid reason, other work is accepted and reintegration becomes merely an academic issue. And of course employees will often simply agree to leave upon receipt of a handsome severance payment.

Changing Location of Work

Companies often change their place of work. Indeed, it is common for multi-nationals to start with a modest investment and increase both the size of their workforce and their investment when commercial success seems assured. This frequently involves transferring both capital and human resources to another location.

Changing the location where people work can create problems under Portuguese law. Article 24 of Decree Law 49,408 (still in force) states that the employer can only transfer an employee to another place of work if such "... transfer does not cause serious prejudice to the worker or if it results from a total or partial transfer of the establishment where the worker in question renders his service".

Take for example a multi-national computer organisation, which has its sales office in one area and its technical assistance department in another. It then decides to transfer the technical assistance department to the site of the sales office. This would be an example of the second part of article 24. However, should this happen, the employee can terminate his contract of employment and demand indemnities unless the employer "... proves that there is no serious prejudice to the employee arising out of such transfer". Let us assume that the computer company has its technical assistance service on the east side of Lisbon and transfers the technicians to the west side of Lisbon to be annexed to the sales office. It takes one hour to cross Lisbon and most technicians live on the east side. Can the employee terminate his contract of employment and claim indemnities?

Perhaps in other countries where there is a dearth of employment such a question would seem academically interesting but of no practical concern. In fact, the invocation of this article in the life of commercial companies has been considerable, as is clearly attested by case law. An example of employee intransigence? No. Experience teaches us that where rights exist they can be used for bargaining purposes. Thus the employee who enjoys his work and is asked to work elsewhere, but feels this to be legally incorrect, is likely to say "yes, but ...". Often, if the request by the employer is incorrect but there are good relations existing between employer and employee the employer will recognise the "illegality" and compensate for this by an increased salary. A happy solution for all.

Nevertheless, when is the transfer legal? The law speaks in general terms and what will constitute "serious prejudice" can be debated at length. Very often, the possibility of a debate can be of benefit to the employer.

Some years ago a major airline had almost all its staff working at Lisbon airport with only a small staff in an office in downtown Lisbon. The company wished to cease operations in Portugal but this necessitated paying substantial indemnities due to the many years of service accrued by many employees. As a strategy, it was decided to request all airport employees to report to work at the downtown office. The company and its lawyers knew in advance that this would be resisted by the airport staff who had lots of "fringe benefits" from working at the airport such as freedom from administrative control, free time, and lax supervision. The employees refused. This had been anticipated and the employees were then notified of disciplinary action which, if successful, would involve dismissal without indemnities. The war of nerves lasted some weeks, the employees arguing that it amounted to a serious prejudice to have to go to downtown Lisbon, and the employer arguing on the contrary that it was a benefit, being far less noisy and more conducive to work.

Eventually, in fear of receiving nothing, reasonable termination payments were made and the airport office closed. The small staff at the downtown office, demoralised by the departure of their colleagues at the airport, also accepted termination pay and the entire operation in Portugal ceased.

One footnote. The law states that the employer "... shall pay for the expenses directly incurred by the employee as a result of the transfer." Does this mean increased bus fares? What if the new area has a higher standard of living and there are no simple restaurants? Or no parking spaces and it is necessary to rent a garage? There is jurisprudence in Portugal to the effect that increased travel expenses can be avoided by changing residence, but often this is not a practical solution.

For the time being, both employer and employee will seek to utilise the existing provisions of the labour law to suit their own best interests.

Acquisition of a Business

A common way of starting a business in another country is to acquire an existing business as a going concern. Obviously, acquiring the shares of the quotas of a Portuguese company changes the internal ownership but leaves intact the entire administrative organisation. The international investor will not generally expect a change in share ownership, even in a closely held family business, to give any special rights to terminate labour contracts. Nor does it. But there are other ways of acquiring a business, and one of them is codified in article 1118 of the Civil Code of Portugal, which speaks of a "trespasse" of a commercial or industrial establishment. Here the purchaser offers to buy, not the shares of the local Portuguese company, but its assets: the land, the machines, equipment, automobiles, trucks, everything but the workers. A "trespasse" implies a selling of the assets of the company, along with its debts, as a unity. In legal theory, what is being sold is a constellation of intangible rights (shown on the balance sheet as assets and liabilities) to a third party. Very often investors believe that by this method of purchase they can separate out the assets from the employees. This is not so. On a trespasse, the seller (obviously) but also the buyer remain liable for all employee obligations which have accrued six months prior to the sale. Notice should be given to the workers so that any claims not yet formalised are brought to the attention of the purchaser.

Employment of Foreigners

Foreigners working in Europe have become accustomed to the idea that work permits are difficult to obtain in many countries and require elaborate procedures. Whether due to the lack of any significant foreign population in Portugal, or to the other influences, foreigners are frequently surprised by the ease with which it is possible to obtain a work permit in Portugal. In fact, addressing the problem simply as a work permit issue is misleading, because this implies, given that most people work, that to live as a foreigner in Portugal you will need a work permit. In fact, living in Portugal by obtaining a residence permit and working in Portugal by obtaining a work permit, are separate but often interrelated problems.

In the first place, there is no prohibition against a foreigner working for himself in Portugal. There is no requirement for permission to work, only permission to reside. The rendering of services as a freelance newspaper writer, or a foreign lawyer, or designing gardens or constructing chalets, none of these examples require a work permit. The situation which requires a work permit is working for someone else with regularity, normally with a fixed hourly duration and being subordinate to the direction of a third party.

But even assuming that it is necessary to have a work permit, that is in the context of an employer–employee relationship, Portuguese legislation allows for companies which have more that five employees to have at least 10% of their staff foreign. Additionally, special circumstances can be invoked where a company exceeds the 10% rule. In these special cases, for example international auditing or management consulting firms, where a high percentage of the staff is non-Portuguese, it has never been difficult to obtain permission from the Ministry of Labour. All that is required is a contract signed between the employer and employee which is sent to the Ministry of Labour for approval.

Individual Tax Issues

The Portuguese Income Tax on Individuals denominated IRS, came into effect at the same time as the income tax on corporate entities, i.e. 1st January 1989. Both tax codes were in response to a need to harmonise Portugal's fiscal system with the rest of Europe and to eliminate many of the tax anachronisms which existed, the most notorious being the segregation of income into different categories, each with its own special rules. This, at least, was the declared intent, but in fact both the individual and corporate income tax codes still have income divided into different categories, and the so-called objective of a "unitary" tax may be questioned. In any event, the 1988 Codes (but effective from 1st January 1989) are a feature of modern economic reality in Portugal and are not likely to suffer substantial changes for some time.

The foreigner investor in Portugal, even if he is an individual, normally comes to do business and hence the relevance of the individual income tax is not as great as the corporate income tax which regulates business income. Nevertheless, many managers of foreign subsidiaries come to Portugal to live for some time and some of the rules applicable to individuals bear reviewing. Perhaps the most important is the consequence of establishing residency. Article 16 of the IRS considers residents those persons who have lived in Portugal more than 183 days, consecutive or not, in a calendar year, or on 31st December of any one calendar year have a residence in Portugal from which the tax authorities may infer that it is intended to be maintained as an "habitual residence". Should any one of these two facts occur, the resident is then subject to tax on worldwide income. In practice, the tax department has not enforced this rule very scrupulously for a variety of reasons, but surely the most obvious is that it would mean that no foreigner would come to live and work in Portugal. The foreign individuals who work in Portugal are taxed on their earned income and I know of no reported cases in the foreign community of the tax department making inquiries as to assets abroad.

Retired people living in Portugal also face a moral dilemma. Normally, those who live in a country as retirees apply for a residence permit. To obtain this permit, they must show means of supporting themselves and in Portugal this can be done by furnishing to the authorities copies of their local (i.e. Portuguese) bank statements indicating funds available or some other source, such as a social security cheque. Interest on bank deposits is taxed and withheld at source and will suffice the tax authorities. For retired people who do not want to open a bank account in Portugal, the declaration of a monthly retirement cheque raises the question whether or not the residence-granting authorities inform the tax authorities. It seems unlikely at present but practices can change overnight. Hence, opening of a bank account seems sensible if at all possible.

The basis for calculating individual income tax permits the deduction of a variety of expenses, including documented medical expenses, and the tax rate is the familiar progressive tax scale. Below are the general IRS tax rates as of 1st January 1993 on net taxable income:

General IRS rates as of 1st January 1993

Taxable Income (Esc. '000)	*Rate (%)*	
	Normal	*(Esc. '000)*
First 860	15	0
More than 860 to 2010	25	+129
More than 2010 to 5160	35	+416.5
Superior to 5160	40%	+1519

However, many categories of income are deductible at source with no further taxes assessed unless the taxpayer chooses to include the income in his tax return and pay on all income the general IRS rates.

IRS Rates Non-Residents

Category of Income Tax	*Withholding Tax Rate (%)*
Royalties	15
Technical assistance	15
Use of equipment	15
Dividends	25
Other securities income	25
Deposit income	20
Other investment income	20
Management functions	25
Gambling winnings	25
Income from real estate, such as rent	15
Capital gains from sale of shares	10
Capital gains on real estate	15-40

IRS Rates Residents

Category of Income Tax	*Withholding Tax Rate (%)*
Royalties	15
Technical assistance	15
Use of equipment	15
Dividends	25
Other securities income	25
Deposit income	20
Other investment income	15
Management functions	15-40
Gambling winnings	25
Income from real estate, such as rent	15
Capital gains from sale of shares	10
Capital gains on real estate	15-40

The above tables are subject to certain important exceptions. Shares held for more than 24 months do not pay any capital gain tax on a sale. Furthermore, capital gains arising from the sale of real estate will pay no tax if the proceeds are reinvested within 24 months provided the real estate sold is used as the family residence and the proceeds are used to purchase another family residence. Regarding corporations, capital gains on the sale of fixed assets will be exempt if proceeds reinvested within two years.

Corporate Tax Issues

The Corporate Portuguese Income Tax Code, called in Portugal IRC, came into effect on 1st January 1989 and represented a completely new codification of the various separate taxes then existing in Portugal. From the perspective of the foreign investor, there are certain tax issues which must be understood and these relate to the manner in which business is to be done in Portugal and the circumstances in which the Portuguese tax laws will be levied on income. Naturally, the corporate tax is levied on income not subject to the personal income tax code and is levied on a commercial, industrial or agricultural activity.

Let us imagine a foreign contractor who wishes to compete for a local Portuguese bid. The question often asked is whether it is necessary to form a local company. Unless required by the contract conditions of the tender, there is no obligation on a foreign investor to form a Portuguese subsidiary. However, the basis for tax purposes is not whether there is a company formed in Portugal but rather whether business is being conducted in Portugal on a systematic basis.

Of course, independently of tax issues, there may be valid reasons for forming a local subsidiary even if it is not necessary to do so. Third parties generally feel more comfortable dealing with a local subsidiary; it has a defined capital. Employees understand more easily for whom they are working. Loans to a local subsidiary will generally be easier to obtain since it is a "Portuguese" company and not a "foreign borrower". But these are all non-tax issues. And if we concentrate only on fundamental tax issues, the foremost question for the foreign investor is the existence or otherwise of a "tax presence".

Basis of Tax

Article 2 of the IRC defines which companies are to be subject to the corporate tax. In conjunction with article 4, a clear understanding can be attained as to the circumstances in which the activities of the foreign investor will be subject to taxation. Companies will be liable to income tax in Portugal when:

- they have their head office or place of effective management in Portuguese territory;
- they fulfil the above criteria, except that they have not achieved full legal status due to an irregularity, e.g. failure to register a company formed before a notary or invalid collective bodies, i.e. a group of people acting as if they had a distinct legal personality but where for some reason there has been a lapse or failure of a fundamental legal obligation;
- they are permanent establishments;
- they conduct any business activity, even if the existence of

an effective management or other type of business presence cannot be proved.

The appropriate legal form in which to carry on business obviously depends on what is taxable and the extent of the tax. Consequently, the next most important relevant section of the IRC is article 4, entitled "Extent of Tax Obligation".

Extent of Tax Obligation

It is important to understand the extent to which sources of income are subject to Portuguese tax. For companies formed in Portugal, the position is clear and far-reaching: income earned *anywhere* will be subject to corporate income tax as Article 4 states that for such companies, IRC is applied to their total income, including income obtained outside the country. For this reason, multi-nationals ordinarily prefer to create separate subsidiaries for different economic markets, so that the tax applicable to each economic market is well defined. In Portugal, there is only the Portuguese income tax. In Angola, another subsidiary is formed, to which only Angolan income tax is applicable.

But article 4 of the IRC speaks of "... corporate bodies ... having their head office or place of effective management in Portuguese territory ...". What does effective management mean? Is this a branch? But if a branch means "effective management", which it surely does in everyday, simple language, no company is going to utilise branch operations in Portugal and subject its worldwide income to Portuguese tax. Consequently, a common-sense understanding of the IRC would suggest that a branch is more closely akin to "a permanent establishment" which only pays tax on income earned in Portugal.

But then, if a branch is not an example of "effective management", what are we to think of the situation where a US corporation forms a wholly owned Portuguese subsidiary, but the whole board of directors of that subsidiary is staffed by the directors of the US corporation. Clearly the US corporation is running the Portuguese subsidiary and yet it defies common sense to think of taxing the worldwide earnings of the US corporation.

Effective management, then, can only mean a company operating in Portugal but which has not gone through any of the formalities required for doing business in Portugal. For example to operate in Portugal a branch must complete certain formalities, e.g. a prior declaration to ICEP, or publication in the local journal, and it is therefore appropriate to follow these formalities in order to classify without any doubt the nature of the business form adopted. We can think of situations where companies sent staff into Portugal with a view to developing the Portuguese market prior to the establishment of a subsidiary. This interpretation is borne out by the preamble to the IRC where the author carefully sets out the theory behind the tax basis:

> "The designation conferred on this tax—tax on the income of collective entities—immediately conveys an understanding as to the ambit of its application. The IRC is applied on all collective entities of public or private law with their head office or place of effective management in Portuguese territory. The point of departure for the definition of taxation was, therefore, the existence of legal personality.
>
> However, entities with their head offices or places of effective management in Portuguese territory which, although lacking legal personality, obtain income ... are equally subject to IRC. Thus entities existing *de facto* are considered to be subject to tax, even when for technical or other reasons an individual attribution is difficult ...".

Although the language quoted is of necessity vague (and probably has to be) we can see the legislators' attempt to tax entities which are doing business in Portugal even where the form in which they are doing business is not easily characterised. It is apparent that the foreign investor should never allow himself to create a business situation of having a site of "effective management" which is not either a local subsidiary or a branch. The entire translation of Article 4 (1) bears this out:

> "In the case of collective bodies and other entities having head offices or effective management in Portuguese territory, IRC is applied to their total income, including income obtained outside the country".

The problem becomes even more complicated when it is understood that a "permanent establishment" is taxed only on income earned in Portugal but no easy distinction is set forth in the IRC between "effective management" and "permanent establishment". In the end, the prudent foreign investor is counselled wisely to set-up a local subsidiary or branch to avoid the problem of tax ambiguity.

In practice a permanent establishment will be considered to exist under article 4 of the IRC if during any 12-month period employees or other contract staff are present in Portugal for a total of not less than 120 days. Consequently, since the permanent establishment is not taxed on worldwide income, it is tempting for the investor who does not form a company to fulfil these requirements in an obvious and demonstrable way. This can most easily be done by going to the Ministry of Finance and filling in the necessary forms declaring in the appropriate form that the investor has set up a permanent establishment.

Branch

A branch, being a permanent establishment, is only taxed on income in Portugal. But to be clearly a permanent establishment and not be confused with a site of "effective management", each with their different tax consequences, branch formalities should be completed. Firstly, the transfer of profits by a branch is not subject to any withholding tax. Additionally interest payments on loans from the head office are also not subject to withholding tax. And in fact, experience has shown that many large corporations do loan money to their subsidiaries, particularly in the early start-up stages. However, as previously indicated, although a branch does offer tax advantages, other practical considerations may become more important in deciding to form a subsidiary.

General Tax Considerations

Portuguese corporate tax law in its generality was modelled on many of the European tax codes, with a view to bringing about the fiscal harmony desired by the EEC.

Some general knowledge of Portuguese corporate tax law will be of assistance to the foreign investor. What is taxed is "taxable profit". This will be the standard accounting items of income, less expenses. In order to bring the submission of Portuguese accounts into a uniform scheme, there was introduced in 1977 the Official Accounting Plan, generally referred to as POC after its Portuguese designation, "Plano Oficial de Contabilidade".

Important to note are the following rules:

(a) IRC, Article 46 permits operating losses to be carried forward for five years but not backwards. There are no loss carry-backs;
(b) capital gains on the sale of fixed assets will be excluded from taxation if the proceeds are reinvested into the "... acquisition, manufacture or construction ..." of other fixed assets within a period of two years from date of sale;
(c) gains on the sale of shares held for more than 24 months are excluded by virtue of Article 10 (2) (c) of IRS;
(d) commercial societies can have their fixed assets revalued should the balance sheet not reflect market conditions. However, this cannot be done unilaterally, but upon application to the tax department; if not, the desired amortisation and depreciation on the new values will not be allowed.
(e) only 60% of a dividend of a company listed on the stock exchange is subject to tax.

The classification of the nature of income earned in Portugal is important as the rates to be applied are dependent on this classification and also whether the taxpayer is resident or non-resident. The results may be summarised in the tables listed below.

IRC Rates Non-Residents

Category of Income Tax	*Withholding Tax Rate (%)*
Royalties	15
Technical assistance	15
Use of equipment	15
Dividends—stock corporation	25
Other securities income	25
Deposit income	20
Other investment income	20
Management functions	25
Gambling winnings	25
Income from real estate	15
Capital gains on fixed assets, but see special rules, p.107 above.	36

IRC Rates Residents

Category of Income Tax	*Withholding Tax Rate (%)*
Royalties	15
Technical assistance	15
Use of equipment	36
Dividends—stock corporation	25
Other securities income	25
Deposit income	20
Other investment income	15
Management functions	20
Gambling winnings	25
Income from real estate	15
Capital gains on fixed assets, but see special rules, p.107 above.	36

Regarding depreciation, the straight-line method is generally used. Rates are provided in tables established by law depending on the specific category of asset. However, Article 28 of the IRC allows other methods of calculating depreciation when the "life of the asset or the economic activity of the company justifies" it.

The general tax rate is 36.5% but in Portugal the local municipalities have the right to levy tax and this varies from municipality to municipality. Probably 40% approximates more closely to the total tax rate.

Of interest to the corporate investor will be the social security tax. Employees discount 11% and the employer pays 24.5% of the gross salary. For purposes of the social security tax, "salary" includes commissions, subsidies, perks, meal tickets (above $675), to name only a few.

Double Tax Treaties

At present there are various double tax treaties with other countries and these are set out in tabular form below. For each country there is shown the amount of tax, depending on the source of income. In many cases, the actual treaty has to be consulted to know which of the alternate taxes will apply.

Country	*Dividends* (%)	*Interest* (%)	*Royalties*
Germany	15	15 or 10	10
Austria	15	10	10 or 5
Belgium	15	15	5
Brazil	15	15	15 or 10
Denmark	15 or 10	15	10
Spain	15 or 10	15	5
Finland	15 or 10	15	10
France	15	12 or 10	5
Italy	15	15	12
Norway	15 or 10	15	10
UK	15 or 10	10	5
Switzerland	15 or 10	10	5

Editor's Note: Where alternate percentage rates are indicated, the treaty in question must be consulted.

Additionally negotiations are often in progress between Portugal and other countries and the investor from a country not listed above should consult the commercial attaché for Portugal in his own country to know if a double tax treaty is imminent.

There is a section at the Ministry of Finance appropriately

entitled "International Tax Department" and there the investor can obtain the forms which, when completed, permit the payment of the treaty tax and the allowance of the relative tax credit at the residence of the taxpayer.

Other Taxes

Portugal has a value added tax modelled on the European VAT systems. The VAT system is consistent with the Sixth and Eighth EEC Directives. Generally speaking, VAT is charged by increasing the sales price of goods or services by the applicable rate and is added to the import value of goods coming into Portugal. VAT is not charged for goods or services which are exported, e.g. where a local Portuguese audit firm supplies services to a company based in London. Most companies both charge VAT and are liable to pay VAT. At the end of the accounting year, VAT payments are offset against VAT receipts. The cost of VAT is of course passed on to the consumer in the final sales price. The most common VAT tax rate is 16%, but there are also rates of 5% (e.g. educational material) and even excessive rates of 30% (e.g. perfumes). Consequently, the VAT tables have to be consulted for any particular category of goods or services.

There are a number of situations creating exemption from VAT but the list is quite long and the Code has to be consulted on a case-by-case basis. They are set forth in Article 9 of the VAT Code and include medical services (but not legal services); educational services; sale of works by the artists; postal services; banking and financial services as to certain operations (the list has to be consulted but it includes granting of credit); insurance services; rendering of services in the area of agriculture.

Companies when opening their accounts at the appropriate fiscal department have to register for VAT (provided the taxable goods or services will exceed an annual invoice value of 800,000 escudos) and the Portuguese Tax Department has computerised a great deal of their services, including VAT. Hence the applicable periods for the payment of instalments of VAT have to be met, otherwise the computerised notice arrives quite promptly.

The VAT tax in theory is easy to calcuate: VAT owed from sales of goods and services less VAT paid on goods and services acquired equals the VAT to be paid or received back.

In addition to VAT, there is a transfer tax of 10% on the sale of real estate above the declared value of 8.1m escudos. There are a number of exemptions from this transfer tax and many of the religious associations operating in Portugal have been able to secure a certificate from the relevant ministry that their association is entitled to an exemption.

Besides the transfer tax, there are many different kinds of legal documents requiring stamps, but the cost of these imposts has never been sufficient to constitute a deterrent to commercial activity by the entrepreneur.

Accounting Treatment of Acquisitions and Mergers

The tax code of Portugal applicable to corporate entities is entitled "Tax Code on Income of Corporate Entities", i.e. corporate income tax (abbreviated as IRC) of which Articles 62 and 63 specifically deal with "mergers and de-capitalisations".

Paragraph 2 of Article 62 exempts from capital gains tax any assets transferred provided their accounting values are not changed. Equally important, Article 63 exempts the partners or shareholders from capital gains provided that as a consequence of the merger the total value attributed to the capital participations has not changed. In simple language, there is no accounting appreciation of each individual share resulting from the merger. We can imagine a shareholder with a 1%

participation in company A, which has a capital of US$1,000,000. Company A merges with company B which has an equal capital. We would then expect the shareholder of the newly formed company resulting from the merger to possess a 0.5% interest in a capital of US$2,000,000 for the provisions of Article 63 to be applicable. Any payments made to the partners as a result of the merger, in addition to the share participation, would be taxable. Additionally, on 21st December 1990, there was enacted Decree Law 403/90 conceding an exemption from the normally applied land transfer tax to companies which proceed to a concentration, the latter including of course a merger. The merger must take place by 31st December 1993 and is granted by a petition to the Ministry of Finance for this purpose.

Additionally, as a result of various fiscal benefits designed to encourage concentrations, it is now possible to obtain the following fiscal incentives in connection with a concentration, namely:

- exemption from real estate transfer tax;
- ability to deduct tax losses of the three previous years;
- exemption from payment of notarial fees.

Doing Business in Portugal: Acquisition or New Company?

How shall the foreign investor do business in Portugal? Shall it be done by acquisition and if so, by assets or purchase of shares? Or should a new company be started? Below I have tried to indicate some conclusions based on my own experience.

Records in Portugal and information concerning the commercial activity of third parties are not developed to the same degree as in other jurisdictions. For example, the concept of chattel mortgage as a recorded fact exists only sparsely in

Portugal and then for items of little significance except to lenders, e.g. cars and boats. When a company borrows money and gives a security interest to a bank, this is done by a private agreement and not recorded anywhere. Consequently, the purchase of a company by shares, or its assets, requires a great deal of investigation, prying out information from employees and managers and following it up with banks. This is time-consumming and not 100% efficient legally. Of course, warranties and declarations can be obtained from responsible managers and most people do conduct business in a fair way, but such philosophical observations do not prevent the ocassional breach of trust. Buying a company in Portugal is not therefore as legally sure as it would be with an extensive recording system.

Furthermore, if we purchase a company, how shall we do it? If the installations are leased, all we can buy are the lease rights and the "economic unit", the going concern, with its assets, liabilities and employees. This is called a "trespass" in Portugal. But we are then confronted with the rule as to transfers of liabilities in Portugal. A creditor has to agree as to the transfer of his credits to another debtor. Any part of the assets transferred, such as security agreements, or reservation of property contracts, requires the approval of the creditor. The transferor normally wants to be released from liability to any banks. This has to be negotiated with each bank. What if we want to change somewhat the line of activity? Will our lease permit this? There exist countless leases in Portugal drafted years ago where the object of the activity was merely "industrial or commercial activity". Are the new purchasers of a tyre-making plant prohibited from making exclusively plastic boats? There is much judicial doctrine in Portugal that a general grant in a lease followed by a specific activity confines the trespass to the same acitivity.

These reservations carry less weight in the case of a subsidiary of a multinational, and the personal guarantee of sellers merits a certain amount of financial recourse.

Assuming, then, that we decide to purchase a company, shall it be done by assets or shall we buy the controlling interests? There is much to be said for purchasing the assets. From the prior rules on transparency previously explored (above), the foreign investor will be greatly hampered when dealing with a public company. It may be necessary to go through an OPA. If we are dealing with a private company, a small share company or quota company, which lies outside the jurisdiction of the S&E Act, then the foreign investor is freer to act but the purchase of shares will not permit any step-up in the value of the assets. Normally share sellers put a price which includes their view of future business. This stepped-up price is not reflected in the asset value on the company balance sheet.

If we cannot take advantage of re-evaluating the balance sheet assets on a share purchase, we are then faced with two alternatives: either we buy the assets or we start a new company. If we buy the assets, we can use our cost for purposes of amortisation and depreciation. But it is the rare company that sells off its assets piecemeal unless it is in trouble. Consequently, invariably, we return to the option of either purchasing an entire company — a trespass — or starting our own company.

Much can be said in favour of starting a new company and experience has shown that, in Portugal at least, this is the normal course of action for the foreign investor. Even where a Portuguese distributorship is bought up or ended, or a joint venture concretised, the preferred method is to create a new company. These general observations, however, are subject to alteration depending on the circumstances.

Final Considerations

Most investors ask a question seldom addressed in legal literature: what is it really like to invest and consequently to work in Portugal? Perhaps traditional legal literature never considers this type of question because it involves a subjective response, an analysis which cannot be proved by reference to any legal source.

Yet this is a real concern for investors and is certainly a relevant concern. An English judge once asked, in a famous case, "how could the laws of the island of Tobago affect English citizens?". By this statement, he gave expression to a common concern of all people. Will we be doing business in an atmosphere conducive to business, are the people friendly, are the laws sensible, is the culture one to be appreciated, is the climate pleasant, are foreigners welcome?

In all these areas Portugal deserves (at least in the opinion of this writer) an unqualified and enthusiastic response. Anyone familiar with the history of Portugal will know that it is a country with a great European tradition and culture, a country hospitable to foreigners (a Portuguese lady married an English king), with laws derived from European sources, a country underpopulated and with a temperate climate.

Valor, the prominent Portuguese economic weekly, recently made the following observations:

> "What can you say then of a country constituted by one, and only one, nation? What can you say of a country which maintains the same stable frontiers for almost 800 years, an absolute world record? What can you say of a country without ethnic questions, regional, lines of friction? You must say it is a very happy country. You must desire it as such and pray to God that it be maintained as such for a good many years, free of dramatic problems that painfully ravage many other regions."

If Portugal as a location for investment offers any drawbacks, they are two, only one of which is curable. Firstly Portugal is a small country and consequently the investor has to think in more modest terms, unless he is using Portugal as a port of entry into the EEC. The other drawback is curable: the Portuguese language, which can be studied and learned. The average learning period, to recognise all common words and speak reasonably well, is about two years. It is a difficult but learned and beautiful language. For those who like to study and speak foreign languages, the Portuguese people are unbelievably encouraging to foreigners struggling to speak their local language. For those who cannot afford the time, English, French and German are spoken by many people, particularly those in the business community, and Spanish is understood by almost everyone. With these closing words, "já não há mais a dizer" (there is nothing more to say).

Index